level

Rehearsing

D

for the Common

Core Standards

Reading

RALLY!
EDUCATION
We're all about student success!®

ISBN 978-1-4204-7896-9

R 7896-9

The following selection used with permission: *I Like It When It's Mizzly* from *I LIKE WEATHER* by Aileen Fisher. Copyright © 1963, 1991 Aileen Fisher. Used by permission of Marian Reiner on behalf of the Boulder Public Library Foundation, Inc.

The following selections Copyright © Highlights for Children, Inc., Columbus, Ohio: *My ~~Stinky~~ Planet-Saving! Summer Vacation* © 2011; *The Song of the Mouse* © 2011; *The Rain Cloud and the Camel* © 2008; *Dazzling Dave Spins Delight* © 2011; *The Dishonest Merchant* © 2000; *Harry Truman, Lost and Found* © 2003; *Stitching the Rip in the Sky* © 2011; *A Game Fit for a President* © 2010; *Living in a Wildlife Camp* © 2011; *I Love the World* © 2011; *I Like It When It's Mizzly* © 2012; *The Dolphin Who Loved Games* © 2009; *Animals and Their Trainers* © 2005; *2,000-Year-Old Homework!* © 2011; *Double Trouble* © 2006; *Learning from a Baby Bear* © 2005; *Alexander's Astounding World Feat* © 2011; *Running Rabbit* © 2000; *Flying Circles Around Mercury* © 2011; *My Favorite Fruit? The Olive!* © 2005; *Benny Benson and the Flag Contest* © 2005; *The View from Camp* © 2006; *Crimson Harvest* © 2009; *Making a Lay-Up* © 2009; *Going in Circles Around Saturn* © 2012; *Fishing for Gold* © 2011; *Little Mo* © 2009.

Photo/Illustration credits: p. 8 & 10 Marcelo Baez; p. 19 Terrence Holekamp; p. 31 Linda Bronson; p. 40 Dave Schulte; p. 42 James Yamasaki; p. 51 & 53 Allan Eitzen; p. 61, 63, & 64 Harry S. Truman Library; p. 76 Katie Flindall; p. 85 Gary Undercuffler; p. 99 Donna Stackhouse; p. 109-112 Tico, Lesley, and Madison McNutt; p. 121 Jesse Reisch; p. 122 David Leonard; p. 131 Lyle Berg; p. 133 & 134 Lincoln Park Zoo; p. 144 Dr. Todd Hickey; p. 145 & 146 David Coulson; p. 155 & 158 Nathan Walker; p. 168 John Rice; p. 169 Charles Fergus; p. 179-181 Paula Becker; p. 182 Allan Eitzen; p. 192 & 195 NASA/Johns Hopkins University Applied Physics Laboratory/ Carnegie Institution of Washington; p. 203 Robert Casilla; p. 227 & 229 Mark Corcoran; p. 239 Ocean Spray Cranberries, Inc.; p. 240 Agricultural Research Service; p. 249 Mark Herreid/123rf.com; p. 251 James Palmer; p. 260 Robert Perdok/dieKleinert/Alamy; p. 263 Tom Powers; p. 271-273 Karen Lee; p. 274-277 Mark Corcoran

0713.MAQ

RALLY! EDUCATION • 22 Railroad Avenue, Glen Head, NY 11545 • (888) 99-RALLY

Contents

*Literary (L), Informational (I), and Paired Passages
with Multiple Choice, Short Response,
Extended Response, and Essay Questions*

Introduction

Rehearsing for the Common Core Standards

Rehearsing for the Common Core Standards: Reading prepares students for the types of tasks, assessments, and tests they may be asked to complete to demonstrate they have the skills listed in the Common Core Reading Standards.

This book includes features expected of Common Core material, including using authentic and complex passages, focusing on close reading and using text-based evidence, and asking complex questions that require students to analyze, critique, and make connections.

Common Core Reading Standards

The Common Core Reading Standards are divided into two parts: Reading Standards for Literature and Reading Standards for Informational Text. These two parts are each divided into three main subtopics, with specific skills listed in each subtopic.

In this book, each subtopic is covered in turn in the first three sections. The final section combines all the subtopics to provide complete coverage of all the skills.

Section	Subtopic	Informational Text Standards Addressed	Literature Standards Addressed
Part A	Key Ideas and Details	Standards 1, 2, and 3	Standards 1, 2, and 3
Part B	Craft and Structure	Standards 4, 5, and 6	Standards 4, 5, and 6
Part C	Integration of Knowledge and Ideas	Standards 7, 8, and 9	Standards 7 and 9
Part D	All Together	All Standards	All Standards

Passage and Question Formats

Each section of the book contains both literary and informational passages, and several sets of paired passages are also included throughout the book. Each passage or set of passages is followed by a set of ten questions. The ten questions cover all the standards of the subtopic, and many questions cover more than one standard.

Rehearsing for the Common Core Standards: Reading includes a range of question types. Each section of the book contains multiple choice, graphic organizer, short response, extended response, and essay questions.

Part A:

Key Ideas and Details

Literary and Informational Passages with Multiple Choice, Short Response, Extended Response, and Essay Questions

Common Core State Standards for Informational Text (Grade 4)

RI.4.1   Refer to details and examples in a text when explaining what the text says explicitly and when drawing inferences from the text.

RI.4.2   Determine the main idea of a text and explain how it is supported by key details; summarize the text.

RI.4.3   Explain events, procedures, ideas, or concepts in a historical, scientific, or technical text, including what happened and why, based on specific information in the text.

Common Core State Standards for Literary Text (Grade 4)

RL.4.1   Refer to details and examples in a text when explaining what the text says explicitly and when drawing inferences from the text.

RL.4.2   Determine a theme of a story, drama, or poem from details in the text; summarize the text.

RL.4.3   Describe in depth a character, setting, or event in a story or drama, drawing on specific details in the text (e.g., a character's thoughts, words, or actions).

Directions: Read the passage. Then answer the questions that follow it.

My ~~Stinky~~ Planet-Saving! Summer Vacation

By Lori Anastasia

1   I chewed on my pencil as I paced back and forth across my bedroom. What was I going to do? It was bad enough that I was the new kid. But now I was sure to get laughed right out of fifth grade. How could my first homework assignment be such a disaster?

2   I sat at my desk and stared at the computer screen. "My name is Anna Kincaid, and this summer I—" I stopped. How could I stand in front of my class and say that I'd spent the entire summer handling something that most people don't even like to talk about? Manure. Otherwise known as poop. I'd spent three months shoveling, collecting, and analyzing cow manure on my grandparents' farm in Oklahoma. I tried to think of a different adventure I could share. Maybe I could say I'd spent the summer on the Weather Control Team preventing tornadoes in the Midwest.

3   "Time for dinner," my mom called.

4   I trudged down the stairs and slid into my chair.

5   "You've been in your room since you got home from school," Mom said. "What are you working on?"

6   I groaned. "I have to tell the class what I did this summer."

7   My younger brother, Seymour, started giggling uncontrollably. "No one will want to sit next to you after they hear you were covered in cow poop all summer!"

8   "OK, that's enough, Seymour," Dad said.

9   "Anna," said Mom, putting green beans in a bowl, "be proud of the work we did this summer. Our planet would be in sad shape without scientists like your grandfather."

10   It's true that my grandfather does important work. Back in 2017, he developed an easy way to use manure as a source of fuel, and he's spent the last couple of decades perfecting the method. Using the manure is now easy, economical, and environmentally safe.

11   "I know, Mom," I said, staring at my meatloaf. "But it's not exactly something people want to hear about before lunch."

12   "Or during dinner," Dad said, chuckling as he also studied his meatloaf.

13   That night I dreamed about more glamorous adventures: scuba diving in Australia as I restored the Great Barrier Reef; swinging from vines as I protected the rain forests in Brazil. I tossed and turned.

14   At school the next day, I hunched over my desk, listening to each kid speak. My palms were sweaty and the knot in my stomach grew tighter. I prepared myself for total humiliation.

15   "And that was my voyage to the moon's first Lunar Hotel and Day Spa," Ember Adams said, finishing her report. She bowed and took her seat.

16   "It's your turn, Anna," Ms. Hammond said.

17   I breathed quickly. Clutching my micro-mobile computer, I stepped to the front of the room and cleared my throat. "This summer I—well, I ..." I stared at the floor. This was my last chance to save my dignity with a tale of fake adventure.

18   Then I thought about Grandpa and how hard he works to save our planet. "I spent the summer collecting cow manure," I blurted.

19   I looked around the room. No one seemed completely disgusted, although there were some confused faces.

20   I hit a few keys on my computer, and a three-dimensional image of a cow eating alfalfa appeared in the middle of the classroom. I proceeded to take my classmates on a virtual tour that started with the cow in the pasture and ended with a man fueling his car at the local methane-gas pump. To my amazement, my classmates were fascinated.

21   Toward the end, I decided to throw in one of Grandpa's corny jokes for good measure. "What did one gas pump say to the other gas pump after an exhausting day of fueling cars?" I paused, then said, "'I'm totally pooped out.'"

22   Laughter and a few good-natured groans filled the room.

23   I finished by saying, "I guess my family's work this summer helped fuel Ember's trip to the moon and Max's underground express train to the deep-sea adventure park."

24   The class applauded as I returned to my desk.

25   The boy seated behind me tapped my shoulder. "Hey, I'm Josh," he said. "I guess you're responsible for my family's agonizing eight-hour road trip to visit my great-aunt Ethel in Maine." He laughed. "Anyway, some of us are playing kickball after school. Want to come?"

26   Who would have thought that I'd make my first friends at this school thanks to Grandpa and my stinky summer vacation—I mean, my fabulous planet-saving adventure!

Directions: Answer the following questions. If you need more space to write an answer, write your answer on your own paper.

1 Why is Anna worried about giving a talk about working with manure?

   A She does not think anyone will believe her.

   B She wants her new classmates to like her.

   C She wants to get a good mark for the assignment.

   D She does not know how to explain the work she did.

2 Read this sentence from paragraph 13.

> *"That night I dreamed about more glamorous adventures: scuba diving in Australia as I restored the Great Barrier Reef; swinging from vines as I protected the rain forests in Brazil."*

What do these examples have in common with the work Anna actually did?

   A They are exciting things to do.

   B They are things to be embarrassed about.

   C They are completed overseas.

   D They are ways of helping the planet.

ATION. No part of this document may be reproduced without written permission from the publisher.

11

3 How does Anna feel in the first paragraph? What details does the author include to show how she feels? Use at least **two** details from the paragraph to support your answer. I the first paragraph Anna feels feels worred. I know this because it states "It was bad enough that I was a new kid." It also mention in the story "But now I was sure to get laughed out of fifth grade. How could my first assignment be such a disater." This evadice shows me Anna was worred because a first homework assignment was such a disater and she was sure to get laughed out of fifth grade.

4 Write a summary of the research that Anna's grandfather does. Explain why manure is an important part of the research. Use details from the story to support your answer. The research that Anna's grandfather does is he is a scientits that studies plants. I know this because it states in the story "Our planet would be in a sad shape without a scientits like your grandfather. The manure is an important part of the research because the grandfather use manure as a source of fuel. I know this because in paragraph ten it states "Back in 2017, he developed an easy way to use manure as a source of fuel, and he's spent the last couple decades to perfecting the method.

5 The story takes place after the year 2017. Complete the chart below by listing **three** details from the story that show it is set in the future.

Details that Show the Future Setting
1) P rk
2)
3)

6 Reread paragraph 14. Explain how the author helps readers imagine how Anna feels. Use at least **two** details from the paragraph to support your answer.

The author helps the reader imagine how Anna feels by using discrption words. I know that because it is using word like.

7 As Anna begins to give her talk, she decides not to tell about a fake adventure. What is the main reason she decides to tell the truth? Use details from the story to support your conclusion.

8 What does Anna telling a joke in paragraph 21 suggest about how she feels? Why is this important to the plot of the story? Use details from the story to support your answer.

9 How is the students' reaction to Anna's speech different from what she expected? Use details from the story to support your answer.

Planning Space

You can complete the chart below to help plan your answer.

Details that Show How Anna Expected Students to React	Details that Show How the Students Actually Reacted

_____

_____

_____

_____

_____

_____

_____

_____

_____

_____

_____

_____

_____

10 Why did Anna spend her summer working with manure? In what way was her summer vacation planet-saving? Use details from the story to support your answer.

Planning Space

You can write notes, make a list, or draw a chart to help plan your answer.

Directions: Read the passage. Then answer the questions that follow it.

The Song of the Mouse

By Cheryl M. Reifsnyder, Ph.D.

1   It's not easy to hear a mouse's voice. Men have low-pitched voices, and kids have high-pitched voices. But mice make ultrasounds, which are too high-pitched for human ears to hear. When Dr. Tim Holy figured out how to listen to male mice, he made an amazing discovery: they sing!

2   Holy is a scientist at the Washington University School of Medicine in St. Louis. Other scientists had shown that male mice produce ultrasounds when they catch the scent of a female. Holy hoped that studying those sounds would help him learn how mice detect and respond to odors.

3   But if Holy wanted to know more about mouse ultrasounds, he needed to change the sounds into some form that he could understand. First he used a computer program to examine "sound pictures." Those pictures looked interesting, with unexpected patterns. He wanted to hear those sounds!

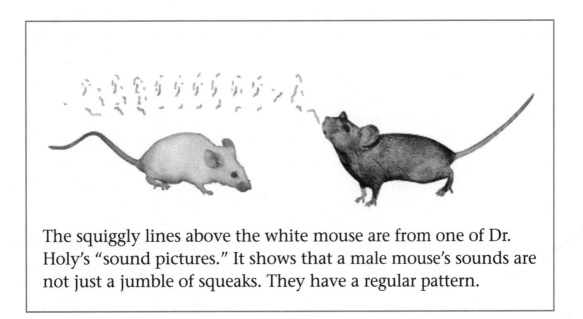

The squiggly lines above the white mouse are from one of Dr. Holy's "sound pictures." It shows that a male mouse's sounds are not just a jumble of squeaks. They have a regular pattern.

Listening to Mice

4   Holy played recordings of the mouse sounds at slow speed. Slowing the sounds also lowers their pitches, changing them from ultrasounds into sounds that human ears can hear. "I joked at the time that they sounded like whale songs," Holy remembered. He wondered: if the recordings were played at normal speed, would the mice be singing?

5   He needed a better way to listen to mouse sounds. What if he used a computer to make the mouse sounds low enough to hear without changing their speed? Holy compared this process to the way a musician can sing the same song starting on a high note or a low note.

6   When Holy played the mouse sounds at their natural speed, they sounded like birdsong. "It was really cool to hear!" he said.

7   Holy was surprised, because most singing creatures are birds, not mammals such as mice. The only mammals known to sing the way birds do are bats and whales.

What Is a Song?

8   Do mice really sing? Lots of animals communicate with sounds, from dogs to crickets to birds. But which animal sounds are true songs? Holy talked to scientists who study birdsong and learned that songs have several things in common.

9   First, true songs are made up of different types of sounds, or syllables, just as words contain different sounds rather than just one repeated sound. For example, a chickadee's song (*chick-a-dee-dee-dee*) has three different syllables: *chick, a,* and *dee*. Do mice make many different types of sounds?

10 To answer this question, Holy used his computer to draw more sound pictures. He experimented with different ways to compare the sounds, and finally he found a pattern.

11 Holy grouped mouse sounds based on how much they jumped in pitch. He identified at least seven different types of syllables—about the same number of syllables as in some birds' songs. He found that mouse sounds contain distinct syllables, the first characteristic of true song.

Songs Have Structure

12 In true songs, the syllables are arranged with a specific structure, not jumbled together. For example, a word makes sense only if the syllables are in the right order. *Crocodile* means something, while *dile-o-croc* does not.

13 Once Holy had figured out how to use the computer to identify different syllables, he looked at sound pictures to see how the mice arranged those syllables. "We wanted to know that they weren't just drawing syllables randomly out of a hat," he said.

14 The result? "Mice tend to repeat themselves with one syllable type and then they'll move on to another," Holy said. Birds often do the same thing. Mouse sounds show structure, the second characteristic of true song.

Songs Are Unique

15 Another characteristic of song is that every animal sings a slightly different song. In fact, individual birds can be identified by their songs. Holy wondered if the same was true for mice.

16 To find out, Holy had to write another computer program. "It gave us a result that I hadn't really expected," he said. He found that different mice preferred to use certain types of syllables. By listening for the syllables, he could identify individual mice by their songs. Mouse sounds are individual, the third characteristic of true song.

17 Mouse sounds contain different syllables, arranged in a structure, and each individual male mouse sings his own song. "When they start singing, sometimes they'll sing for 10 minutes," Holy added. Mice really, truly sing.

Understanding Songs

18 Now Holy and other scientists have a list of other questions about mouse songs. Do male mice sing to attract females? Do female mice sing, too? How do mice learn to sing?

19 Holy and his lab will try to answer some of these questions. That's his favorite part of science. "You get to spend your time trying to figure out how the world works," he said. "To me, that's the best job there could possibly be."

Directions: Answer the following questions. If you need more space to write an answer, write your answer on your own paper.

11 Which statement is the best summary of the article?

   A A scientist does experiments to find out why mice sing.

   B A scientist makes an interesting new discovery about mice.

   C A scientist tries to communicate with mice.

   D A scientist uses songs to identify different mice.

12 Which detail is included in the article to help explain that songs are made up of different types of sounds?

   A Mice make sounds that are too high-pitched for humans to hear.

   B A chickadee's song has the three syllables *chick*, *a*, and *dee*.

   C The word *crocodile* has meaning, but *dile-o-croc* does not.

   D Mice sometimes keep singing for 10 minutes.

13 Explain why Dr. Tim Holy began his research. Was he expecting to hear mice sing? Use details from the article to support your answer.

14 The article suggests that Holy's findings surprised scientists. Give **two** details from the article that are included to show why it was a surprising finding.

©RALLY! EDUCATION. No part of this document may be reproduced without written permission from the publisher.

15 Look closely at the diagram and read the caption. Which quality of true song does the diagram show that the mouse sounds had? Use details from the article to support your answer.

16 Read this quote from paragraph 4 of the article.

"I joked at the time that they sounded like whale songs,"
Holy remembered.

How does Holy probably feel about making this joke now? Use details from the article to support your conclusion.

17 Dr. Tim Holy used computer programs to complete his research. Complete the graphic organizer below by describing **two** problems Holy had and how he used a computer program to solve each problem.

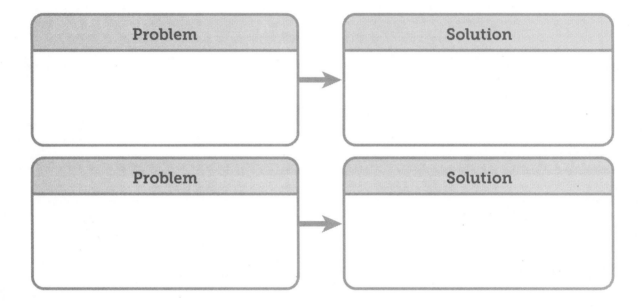

Problem	Solution

Problem	Solution

18 In "Listening to Mice," the author explains that Holy slowed the speed of the recordings so he could hear them. Why did Holy then need a better way to listen to the sounds? Use details from the article to support your answer.

19 Dr. Tim Holy concluded that mice sing after comparing the sounds to the characteristics of song. Describe the **three** characteristics of song and explain how the mouse sounds met each characteristic. Use details from the article to support your answer.

Planning Space

You can complete the table below to help plan your answer.

Mouse Sounds and the Characteristics of Song

Characteristic of Song	How Mouse Sounds Meet the Characteristic

_____

_____

_____

_____

_____

_____

_____

_____

_____

_____

_____

_____

20 Discoveries in science are often made by asking and answering questions. Explain why Holy's research is a good example of this. Use at least **three** details from the article to support your answer.

Planning Space

You can write notes, make a list, or draw a chart to help plan your answer.

_____

_____

_____

_____

_____

_____

_____

_____

_____

_____

_____

_____

Directions: Read the passage. Then answer the questions that follow it.

The Rain Cloud and the Camel

By Lori Mortensen

1   Said the rain cloud to the camel,
     "Why don't you move away?
     The desert's such a prickly place.
     Why would you want to stay?

2   "Come with me and you will see
     Where dandelions grow,
     Where water sparkles in the streams,
     And gentle breezes blow."

3   Said the camel to the rain cloud,
     "Thanks for stopping by.
     The desert *is* a prickly place
     With seasons long and dry.

4   "But I would rather stay right here,
     Where the sun shines warm and bright,
     Where sandy dunes flow like the sea,
     And stars fill up the night.

5   "Still, as you float through endless skies,"
     Said the camel with a wink,
     "I'm always glad each time you come
     To share a rainy drink."

Directions: Answer the following questions. If you need more space to write an answer, write your answer on your own paper.

21 Which inference do the rain cloud's words in the first stanza best support?

A He has never seen a desert before.

B He feels sorry for the camel.

C He has been all over the world.

D He wants to make the camel feel bad.

22 Why does the camel decide to stay in the desert?

A He is too afraid to leave.

B He thinks the rain cloud is lying.

C He can live without water.

D He enjoys living there.

23 Why does the rain cloud call the desert a "prickly place"? Use details from the poem to support your answer.

24 Compare the place the rain cloud describes in the second stanza with a desert. Include at least **two** examples of how a desert is different.

25 The poem describes a conversation between a rain cloud and a camel. Do you think the conversation would have changed the rain cloud's opinions about living in the desert? Use details from the poem to support your conclusion.

26 The camel knows that the desert has both good and bad points. Complete the chart below to summarize what the camel likes and dislikes about living in the desert.

Life in the Desert

Good Points	Bad Points
1)	1)
2)	2)
3)	3)

27 How would the camel most likely sound when he speaks in the last stanza? Explain how this helps show how the camel feels about the desert. Use details from the poem to support your answer.

28 Read this common saying.

Don't judge a book by its cover.

Which character in the poem does the lesson of this saying most relate to? Explain your choice.

29 In the second stanza, the rain cloud describes a place that he likes. In the fourth stanza, the camel describes a place that he likes. Describe how the language used by each character shows how they feel about the place described. Use specific examples of the language used in each stanza to support your answer.

Planning Space

You can complete the chart below to help plan your answer.

Example of Language in the Second Stanza	What the Language Suggests

Example of Language in the Fourth Stanza	What the Language Suggests

_____

_____

_____

_____

_____

_____

_____

_____

_____

_____

_____

_____

_____

30 How does the poem show the importance of making the most of what you have? Use details from the poem to support your answer.

Planning Space

You can write notes, make a list, or draw a chart to help plan your answer.

_____

_____

_____

_____

_____

_____

_____

_____

_____

_____

_____

_____

Directions: Read the passage. Then answer the questions that follow it.

Dazzling Dave Spins Delight

By Cheryl Weibye Wilke

1   Wherever you see Dazzling Dave, you're likely to see him walk the dog, skin the cat, and split the atom. Dave Schulte is a professional yo-yo performer. He spins about 13,000 yo-yo tricks each year. He performs about 130 shows annually, teaching children around the world how to yo-yo.

2   Dave started to yo-yo when he was in college. "I was stressed out during a week of tests when my neighbor stopped by and said, 'Hey, this will help.' I picked up his yo-yo for relief, but *then* I really wanted to figure it out. It was challenging!"

Yo-Yo Teacher

3   After college, Dave taught middle-school students. But he couldn't get the yo-yo off his mind and out of his hands. So he left teaching to yo-yo full time. Soon, he discovered that he still had a passion for teaching.

4   So Dave became a yo-yo teacher! He teaches how to yo-yo, of course. But he also teaches the fundamentals of physics and why things spin.

5   Dave says the main skill needed to become good at yo-yoing is hand-eye coordination. "Juggling and sports such as baseball and lacrosse are great activities to work on that."

6   When he first started to yo-yo, Dave learned hundreds of new tricks each year. "I was yo-yoing eight hours a day." The first trick Dave remembers really working at was called the Star. It took him two or three days to learn it. Now, he says, "I learn about one new trick a month. But they're super-duper tough tricks."

7   Who's coming up with all the new tricks? "Kids from ages 10 to 16 who are getting into the yo-yo," says Dave, grinning. "One of my biggest challenges is keeping up with the new 'school tricks'— tricks developed almost daily by creative kids who have time to work with the yo-yo."

Yo-Yo Master

8   As in most sports, practice, practice, practice does make perfect. Dave is a National Yo-Yo Master. It's the highest honor in this sport. There are only 13 National Yo-Yo Masters in the world. They are chosen for their skill with the yo-yo and for their hard work to promote the yo-yo in their communities. Now that's dazzling!

Do You Yo-Yo?

9   All you need to yo-yo is ... a yo-yo! Dave recommends getting one that unscrews so that you can untangle knots.

10   Once you have selected your yo-yo, customize it to your height. Begin by holding the yo-yo between your feet on the floor. Raise the string and tie an overhand knot level with your belly button. Cut off the excess string. Make a slipknot for the middle finger of your throwing hand. Dave suggests changing the string after four to six hours of yo-yo playing time, or if it's dirty or worn.

11   Finally, Dave recommends joining or forming a yo-yo club. The best way to learn, he says, is hands-on. Go to your public library for books and videos.

Tip

12   Hold the yo-yo in your hand with your palm up. Make sure that the string is looped around your middle finger and goes over the top of the yo-yo.

Got Your Yo-Yo? Now Let's Go!

Throwdown

Curl up your arm as if you're making a muscle.

Bring your elbow down with a snap and release the yo-yo as it goes over the ends of your fingers.

Then turn your hand over to catch the yo-yo upon return.

Sleeper

Start with a Throwdown.

Leave the yo-yo spinning at the bottom of the string.

Before it slows down too much, turn your hand over (palm down) and give the string a slight upward jerk to return the yo-yo to your hand.

Walk the Dog

Throw a fast Sleeper. Gently lower the yo-yo to the floor so that it barely touches.

Don't bounce your hand. The yo-yo will begin to move along the floor.

Directions: Answer the following questions. If you need more space to write an answer, write your answer on your own paper.

31 Which sentence best supports the idea that teaching yo-yo involves science?

A "He spins about 13,000 yo-yo tricks each year."

B "He performs about 130 shows annually, teaching children around the world how to yo-yo."

C "But he also teaches the fundamentals of physics and why things spin."

D "Dave says the main skill needed to become good at yo-yoing is hand-eye coordination."

32 What is the main purpose of the information in paragraph 2?

A to explain one of the main benefits of using yo-yos

B to describe how Dave got started using a yo-yo

C to warn that learning the yo-yo is difficult at first

D to suggest that people of all ages can enjoy yo-yoing

33 In the first sentence, what do the terms "walk the dog," "skin the cat," and "split the atom" refer to? Use details from the article to support your answer.

34 The article describes how Dave yo-yos as a career. Has Dave been successful in his career? Use at least **two** details from the article to support your answer.

35 Use details from the article to support the conclusion that yo-yoing well requires patience. Use at least **two** details from the article in your answer.

36 How are the tricks Dave learns today different from the tricks he learned when he first started? Describe at least **two** differences in your answer.

37 How are all the tricks described in "Got Your Yo-Yo? Now Let's Go!" related? Explain why it would be important to learn the tricks in order. Use details from the article to support your answer.

38 Compare and contrast how to do the tricks Sleeper and Walk the Dog. Describe **one** way the tricks are similar and **one** way they are different. Use details from the article to support your answer.

39 Even though a yo-yo is simple, yo-yoing can be challenging. Describe the **two** main factors that make yo-yoing challenging. Use details from the article to support your answer.

Planning Space

You can write notes, make a list, or draw a chart to help plan your answer.

_____

_____

_____

_____

_____

_____

_____

_____

_____

_____

_____

_____

_____

40 The article states that yo-yo masters are chosen "for their skill with the yo-yo and for their hard work to promote the yo-yo in their communities." Explain how Dave meets both these measures. Use details from the article to support your answer.

Planning Space

You can write notes, make a list, or draw a chart to help plan your answer.

_____

_____

_____

_____

_____

_____

_____

_____

_____

_____

_____

_____

_____

Directions: Read the passage. Then answer the questions that follow it.

The Dishonest Merchant
A Romanian Legend

Retold by David Roper

1 Once upon a time, a prince known for his intolerance of dishonesty ruled in Romania. During his reign, a greedy merchant from another country traveled through the land.

2 During one journey, the merchant lost a bag containing one thousand Romanian coins called *lei*. Each time the merchant came to a crossroads, he told everyone that he would give one hundred lei to anyone who found the money.

3 Not long afterward, a peasant found the bag. He was an honest man, and he hastened to find the merchant.

4 "I found this bag behind the fish market at the crossroads near my home," the peasant said to the merchant.

5 The merchant trusted no one, so he went aside to count the money. To his surprise, all one thousand coins were still in the bag. He was happy to have his money back, but he was also saddened by the thought of giving some of it away. He wondered how he could get out of his promise and still appear to be fair.

6 At last he went back to the peasant. "I thank you for returning my money," he said. "I notice that you have already taken your reward, for there were only nine hundred coins in the bag."

7 The peasant protested. "But I did not even open the bag before I gave it to you!"

8 The merchant ignored the peasant's words. "I hope you enjoy your reward," he said. "Thank you again and good-bye." He quickly departed.

9 The peasant was upset—not just because he had received no reward but because he had been accused of taking money without permission. He hurried to the palace and requested to see the prince. He told his sad story, and the prince promised that he would uncover the truth.

10 The prince sent word for the merchant and the peasant to appear before him on a certain day. He told the merchant to bring the bag of money.

11 When the day arrived, the merchant told his side of the story and the peasant told his. As the prince listened, it became obvious to him that the peasant was telling the truth.

12 When they had finished, the prince said to the merchant, "You lost a bag with one thousand coins. Is that correct?"

13 "Yes," said the merchant.

14 The prince took the money bag, which now held only nine hundred lei. "And when you were handed this bag, it contained only nine hundred coins?"

15 "That is true," said the merchant, trying to look sincere.

16 "I am sure that you are telling the truth," said the prince, "for nothing is punished so severely in this court as dishonesty. However, these facts present me with a problem."

17 The prince held up the bag for all to see. It was an ordinary leather bag, like thousands of others. He asked the merchant, "If your bag contained one thousand coins and this bag has only nine hundred, then how do you know this is your bag?"

18 The merchant had trouble speaking. "I ... I," he stammered. Then he was silent.

19 The prince continued. "It is obvious that this is not your bag. My verdict therefore is that you should continue to inquire at crossroads until you find your bag with one thousand lei. I wish you well in your quest."

20 The prince turned to the peasant. "And I decree that you take care of this bag of nine hundred coins until the rightful owner comes forth. If we do not find the owner within three months, then the money will be yours as a reward for your honesty."

21 There was nothing more to say, since there could be no appeal regarding the prince's verdict. The dishonest merchant and the honest peasant left the prince's chamber, the first very sad and the other very happy.

22 Thus was dishonesty treated in the days of the prince.

Directions: Answer the following questions. If you need more space to write an answer, write your answer on your own paper.

41 What main quality of the merchant causes him to choose not to give the reward?

A   jealousy

B   impatience

C   greed

D   laziness

42 Read this sentence from the story.

> *"The peasant was upset—not just because he had received no reward but because he had been accused of taking money without permission."*

This sentence is mainly included to show that the peasant

A   has pride

B   is determined

C   has a short temper

D   trusts people too easily

43 The outcome for the merchant offers readers a lesson about

A   being prepared

B   keeping your promises

C   working hard

D   asking others for help

44 In paragraph 16, the prince says that he is sure the merchant is telling the truth. Does the prince mean what he says? Use at least **two** details from the story to support your answer.

45 Read this sentence from paragraph 17.

"It was an ordinary leather bag, like thousands of others."

Why is this detail important to the plot of the story? Use details from the story to support your answer.

46 How does the merchant feel when the prince asks him how he can know it is his bag? Use at least **two** specific details from the story to support your answer.

47 The prince says that the peasant can keep all the coins if the rightful owner does not come forward. How can you tell that the rightful owner will not come forward? Use details from the story to support your answer.

48 The merchant does not give the reward because he does not want to lose one hundred coins. How does the ending of the story make this decision seem amusing? Use details from the story to support your answer.

49 If the same events happened again, which main character do you think would be most likely to act differently? Use details from the story to explain why you chose either the peasant or the merchant.

50 The outcome of the story is described in paragraphs 19 to 21. How do the merchant's and the peasant's actions at the beginning lead to the final outcome? Explain whether the outcome is fair for the peasant and the merchant. Use information from the story to support your answer.

Planning Space

You can complete the charts below to help plan your answer.

Merchant's Actions

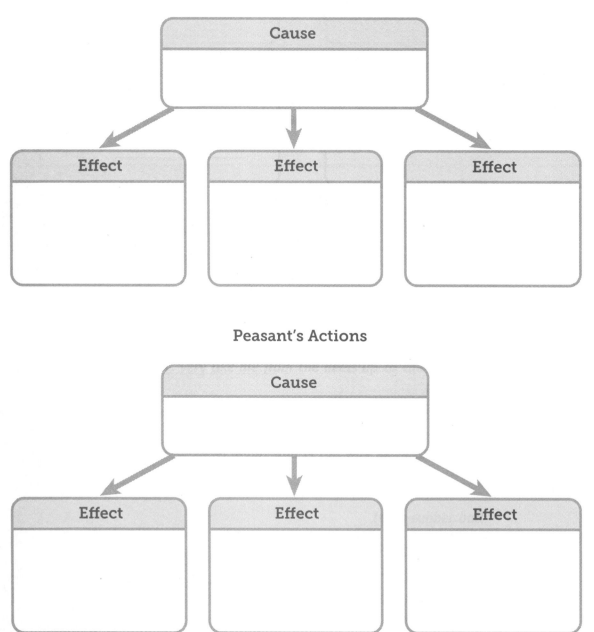

Peasant's Actions

_____

_____

_____

_____

_____

_____

_____

_____

_____

_____

_____

_____

_____

_____

_____

_____

_____

_____

_____

_____

_____

_____

_____

_____

_____

Directions: Read the passage. Then answer the questions that follow it.

Harry Truman, Lost and Found

By Janice Jump

1 In 1892, children seldom wore glasses, but eight-year-old Harry S. Truman was different. He was probably the only one in his class to have spectacles.

2 Harry's mother, Martha, had noticed something odd about his eyesight. Harry was a very early reader and spent much time reading the large-print family Bible. But he couldn't make out smaller print or see anything from a distance.

3 At a Fourth of July celebration, everyone watched the exploding fireworks except Harry. He jumped when the rockets blasted but was unable to see them.

4 Martha Ellen Truman realized her son needed help. She hitched up her horses and took Harry to an eye specialist. The doctor diagnosed Harry's condition as "flat eyeballs" and fitted him with thick lenses. He warned Harry to be careful and told him not to get involved in any rough play.

5 Harry's spectacles opened a new world for him.

6 "When I first put the glasses on I saw things and saw print I'd never seen before," he later said.

7 Harry loved history. His favorite books were *Great Men and Famous Women*, a four-volume set edited by Charles Francis Horne, a gift from his mother on his twelfth birthday.

8 Harry was teased and called "sissy" because he spent so much time reading. His mother insisted that fighting was for babies, so Harry resisted the temptation and went to the library instead.

9   "I was too busy reading books to be bad," Truman later said. "I'd read all three thousand books in the library by the time I was fourteen years old."

10 Reading wasn't Harry's only interest. He also wanted to play baseball. But Harry's mother didn't want him to play sports. She was afraid he might break his expensive glasses. Harry figured out a way to make it happen. When a neighborhood baseball game started, he volunteered to be the umpire, knowing his glasses would be safely hidden under his umpire mask.

11 Throughout his life, Harry was always concerned about his glasses. Lucky for him, good fortune followed him and his glasses. On three dangerous occasions at different times in his life, Harry Truman and his glasses escaped safe and sound.

Soldier Truman

12 In 1917 the United States entered World War I. At the age of thirty-three, Harry became a lieutenant in the U.S. Army. He took along three extra pairs of glasses when he left for France.

13 During maneuvers against the German forces, his horse, Dobbin, rode too close to a low-hanging branch. Harry's glasses were brushed off. He glanced down the path, but they had vanished. There was no time to fetch his extra pair from the supply wagon. Harry was frantic. He was in the middle of a battle, and he was as blind as a bat.

14 Then he spied something shining on his horse's rump. It was his glasses!

Senator Truman

15 In 1935 Harry S. Truman became a U.S. senator. During his six-year term, he and his family traveled to their home in Independence, Missouri, to spend summer vacations.

16 On one trip, the family was involved in an automobile accident. Senator Truman was wearing his glasses, but he couldn't see the stop sign.

17 It was blocked by a parked car. He drove through the intersection, and another car crashed into them.

18 The car suffered extensive damage, but Senator Truman and his wife, Bess, suffered only minor injuries. His daughter, Margaret, was safe in the back seat.

19 The senator's glasses were found on the floor—without a scratch! He had flung them over his shoulder in a desperate attempt to save them.

President Truman

20 On April 12, 1945, Harry S. Truman became the thirty-third President of the United States. After being elected to a second term, President Truman took his family on a vacation to Key West, Florida.

21 President Truman and his daughter went to the beach. Harry jumped into the water and coaxed her to follow, but Margaret sat on the seawall and watched.

22 Suddenly a large wave knocked Truman over, and under he went. The Secret Service men came to the rescue.

23 President Truman was fine, but his glasses were gone!

24 Truman had extra pairs in his room, but the Secret Service insisted upon looking for them. Unfortunately, they couldn't find the President's glasses.

25 Later, Truman sat on the seawall and relaxed. He noticed a patch of light on the sandy beach. Truman summoned the Secret Service men, and they investigated. It was his glasses. They had been washed up by the tide.

In almost every picture of Harry S. Truman you'll notice he's wearing glasses. There is a rare exception—Truman's face on the photograph used on his army AEF (American Expeditionary Forces) Identity Card when he was a captain.

The photograph shows Truman from the waist up. One can only guess that Truman was holding his glasses.

Directions: Answer the following questions. If you need more space to write an answer, write your answer on your own paper.

51 Which sentence from the article best summarizes the main idea?

A "In 1892, children seldom wore glasses, but eight-year-old Harry S. Truman was different."

B "The doctor diagnosed Harry's condition as 'flat eyeballs' and fitted him with thick lenses."

C "His mother insisted that fighting was for babies, so Harry resisted the temptation and went to the library instead."

D "On three dangerous occasions at different times in his life, Harry Truman and his glasses escaped safe and sound."

52 In paragraph 9, Truman is quoted saying, "I'd read all three thousand books in the library by the time I was fourteen years old." Why is this quote important in the article?

A It emphasizes his love for books.

B It suggests that he had few friends.

C It explains how he learned about history.

D It indicates why he was successful in his life.

53 Read these sentences from the end of the article.

"The photograph shows Truman from the waist up. One can only guess that Truman was holding his glasses."

What is the author implying in these sentences?

A Truman's glasses were so important to him that he was probably not actually without them.

B Truman would have preferred not to wear glasses, but recognized that he needed them.

C Truman was lucky often, but probably lost his glasses at least once.

D Truman was always prepared, so often had a spare pair of glasses with him.

54 Harry needed glasses as a boy because of his poor eyesight. How does the author emphasize how poor Harry's eyesight was? Use at least **two** specific examples from the article to support your answer.

55 Read the anecdote about Harry playing baseball in paragraph 10. What does the anecdote reveal about Harry's character? Use details from the article to support your answer.

56 In paragraph 5, the author states that Harry's spectacles "opened a new world for him." Explain what this "new world" was and why it was important to Harry. Use details from the article to support your answer.

57 How does Harry's childhood help explain how much his glasses meant to him later in life? Use details from the article to support your answer.

58 Summarize the lucky event described in the section "Soldier Truman." Why was it so important for Harry to get his glasses back? Use details from the article to support your answer.

59 The title of the article is "Harry Truman, Lost and Found." Explain how this title summarizes the main idea of the article. Use details from the article to support your answer.

60 The article describes three "dangerous occasions" where Harry S. Truman was lucky not to lose his glasses. Explain why each event was lucky. Which event do you feel involved the most luck? Which event would have been most dangerous if he had lost his glasses? Use information from the article to support your answer.

Planning Space

You can complete the chart below to help plan your answer.

	Why was the event lucky?	How lucky was the event?	Would losing the glasses be dangerous?
Event in "Soldier Truman"			
Event in "Senator Truman"			
Event in "President Truman"			

_____

_____

_____

_____

_____

_____

_____

_____

_____

_____

_____

_____

_____

Part B:

Craft and Structure

*Literary, Informational, and Paired Passages with Multiple Choice,
Short Response, Extended Response, and Essay Questions*

Common Core State Standards for Informational Text (Grade 4)

RI.4.4 Determine the meaning of general academic and domain-specific words or phrases in a text relevant to a grade 4 topic or subject area.

RI.4.5 Describe the overall structure (e.g., chronology, comparison, cause/effect, problem/solution) of events, ideas, concepts, or information in a text or part of a text.

RI.4.6 Compare and contrast a firsthand and secondhand account of the same event or topic; describe the differences in focus and the information provided.

Common Core State Standards for Literary Text (Grade 4)

RL.4.4 Determine the meaning of words and phrases as they are used in a text, including those that allude to significant characters found in mythology (e.g., Herculean).

RL.4.5 Explain major differences between poems, drama, and prose, and refer to the structural elements of poems (e.g., verse, rhythm, meter) and drama (e.g., casts of characters, settings, descriptions, dialogue, stage directions) when writing or speaking about a text.

RL.4.6 Compare and contrast the point of view from which different stories are narrated, including the difference between first- and third-person narrations.

Directions: Read the passage. Then answer the questions that follow it.

Stitching the Rip in the Sky

A Polish Folktale Retold by Ellen L. Ramsey

1   There once was a tailor so thin that people would say, "He could fit through the eye of his needle!" He ate only noodles and eels that slid and slithered down his very thin throat.

2   This tailor was known for his fine stitchery and great kindness. He was as happy to mend a child's mitten for no money as to mend a lady's ball gown for a silver coin.

3   One day, the town's wisest woman limped into the tailor's shop.

4   "Tailor," she said, "will you stitch up the cut in my foot?"

5   The tailor tried not to cringe, for he could see the woman's pain. He nodded with sympathy. "My needle and thread are at your disposal."

6   As he stitched, the wise woman spoke. "Tailor, you must travel west to the town of Pacanow, where a princess weeps and the people are in danger. Help this town, and you will win a reward more golden than gold."

7   "More golden than gold?" the tailor asked. "How can that be?"

8   "No time for questions," the wise woman said. "You must leave immediately."

9   The tailor packed pins and needles, then tucked spool after spool of thread into his pockets.

10 It was an extraordinarily blustery day. The wind popped buttons off coats and jackets. The tailor often stopped to sew on buttons for the people he met. As he drew nearer to Pacanow, it started to rain—a pelting, pouring rain, as if thousands of spigots in the sky had been turned on. The tailor pulled his jacket over his head and kept walking.

11 When he reached Pacanow, a throng of sopping-wet people stood in the town square. "What brings you out in this dreadful storm?" the tailor asked.

12 "Our great king died nine days ago," a man said. "The same day, this terrible rain started. The princess has been unable to leave her room until today. And now she is issuing a proclamation."

13 Trumpets blared. The princess, who was very tall, appeared in mourning clothes. "I grieve for my father, the king," she said. "But I also fear for the town. Rain has gushed down chimneys and put out hearth fires. It is causing crops to rot in the fields. If it doesn't stop, we will be swept away by the waters. I offer a golden reward to the person who stops this dreadful rain."

14 The crowd stood sad and soggy—and silent.

15 The tailor looked into the pleading eyes of the princess. He stepped forward. "Don't despair. I'll think of a way to stop the rain."

16 "Come with me to the castle," the princess said, "and we will think together as we eat any meal you desire."

17 The tailor and the princess sat in the dining room, where they thought and talked and ate noodles and eels. Watching the rain fall in sheets, they arrived at the same conclusion: "There must be a gigantic hole in the sky!"

18 "With my needle and thread, I will stitch up the hole!" cried the tailor.

19 The princess called out to the townspeople, "Bring all of your ladders and thread!"

20 The tailor and the townspeople tied the ladders together into one long ladder. Grunting and groaning, they hoisted it high into the sky until it leaned against a cloud.

21 Then the tailor, with needle in hand and pockets stuffed with thread, climbed up ... and up ... and up ... until he reached the hole in the sky.

22 The tailor stitched and stitched. When he was almost finished repairing the hole, he realized that he could not reach its top corner.

23 "Alas," said the tailor, standing tiptoe on the ladder's highest rung, "I am not tall enough to reach the very top corner!"

24 "Don't despair," called the princess. She climbed up … and up … and up. She was just tall enough to stitch the final stitch and knot the end of the thread.

25 As the tailor and the princess descended, the sun shone brightly and the townspeople cheered.

26 At the bottom of the ladder, the princess said, "Thank you, tailor, for saving our town. I will gladly grant you the reward I promised—a bag of gold."

27 "Thank you, princess, for helping me save your town," said the tailor. "But the reward I desire is more priceless than gold. I humbly ask for your hand in marriage."

28 The princess smiled. "That is a request I will gladly grant."

29 Thus the tailor received a reward more golden than gold, as the wise old woman had foretold.

30 At their wedding, the very thin tailor and the very tall princess danced in clothes stitched with golden threads. And such was the joy of the celebration that the entire town glowed in a light even brighter than gold.

Directions: Answer the following questions. If you need more space to write an answer, write your answer on your own paper.

61 In paragraph 1, why does the author describe how people say that the tailor "could fit through the eye of his needle"?

    A to explain why the tailor is good at sewing

    B to emphasize how thin the tailor is

    C to suggest that the tailor has magic powers

    D to highlight how much the tailor enjoys his work

62 Which phrase in paragraph 5 best shows that the tailor found the woman's cut horrible?

    A "tried not to cringe"

    B "nodded with sympathy"

    C "needle and thread"

    D "at your disposal"

63 The author uses words and phrases to show how heavy the rain was. Complete the web below by listing **three** more specific examples of the language used to emphasize how heavy the rain was.

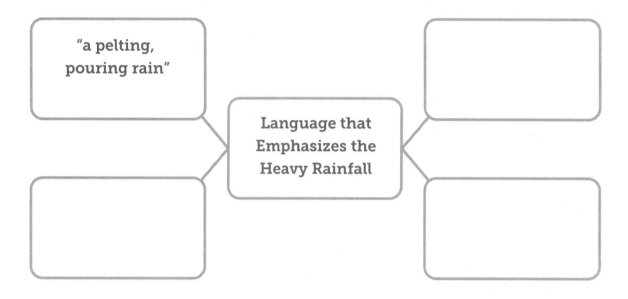

"a pelting, pouring rain"

Language that Emphasizes the Heavy Rainfall

64 Reread paragraphs 6 to 8. How does the dialogue in these paragraphs advance the plot? Use details from the story to support your answer.

65 Read these sentences from the story.

> *"This tailor was known for his fine stitchery and great kindness. He was as happy to mend a child's mitten for no money as to mend a lady's ball gown for a silver coin."*

Describe the relationship between the two sentences. Use details from the sentences to support your answer.

66 Describe **two** things you learn from the speech the princess gives in paragraph 13. Explain why what she says is important. Use details from the story to support your answer.

67 Explain the meaning of the phrase "pleading eyes" in paragraph 15. How does this detail help explain why the tailor agrees to help? Use details from the story to support your answer.

68 In paragraph 29, the author uses rhyme. What feeling does the rhyme help create? How does this relate to the plot of the story? Use details from the story to support your answer.

69 Alliteration is the use of repeating sounds in neighboring words. The author uses alliteration throughout the story. Give **three** examples of alliteration and explain why the author used each one.

Planning Space

You can complete the table below to help plan your answer.

Use of Alliteration

Example	Purpose

_____

_____

_____

_____

_____

_____

_____

_____

_____

_____

_____

_____

70 The story is told from a third-person point of view. Think about how the story would be different if it was told from a first-person point of view. Give **two** examples of scenes where the emotion of the tailor would be clearer if the story was told from his point of view. Use details from the story to support your answer.

Planning Space

You can write notes, make a list, or draw a chart to help plan your answer.

_____

_____

_____

_____

_____

_____

_____

_____

_____

_____

_____

Directions: Read the passage. Then answer the questions that follow it.

A Game Fit for a President

By Holly D. Yount

1   *Bert twists his upper body, gathers his strength, and hurls the ball back toward the opposing team.*

2   *Back and forth the ball goes. Sweat rolls down the players' faces as each three-man team scrambles to get under the ball and catch it on the fly. One thought is on their minds: don't let the ball touch the ground.*

3   *The distant sound of a factory whistle blows, ending the game. Bert's team wins, but the men will be back in the morning for a rematch.*

4   Bert isn't just any player. He is Herbert Hoover, President of the United States. The ball field isn't ordinary either. It is the neatly trimmed White House lawn.

5   And the game? Hoover-ball.

6   Herbert Hoover didn't always like to exercise, but he did like to be healthy.

7   After his 1928 election, President Hoover noticed he had gained weight. "Getting daily exercise to keep physically fit is always a problem for Presidents. Once the day's work starts there is little chance to walk, to ride, or to take part in a game," Hoover admitted. Still the extra 20 pounds were enough to make him talk to his doctor, Admiral Joel T. Boone, about a fitness program.

8   Hoover mentioned a game called bull-in-the-ring. He had played it on the battleship *Utah* with the ship's crew during a goodwill trip to South America. Players form a circle around one person. The player in the middle—or the "bull"—is it. Players toss an eight-pound ball to each other while the bull tries to catch it.

The Game Begins!

9   Admiral Boone took parts of three games—bull-in-the-ring, tennis, and volleyball—to create a new sport. At first, Hoover didn't think anyone would join him at 7:00 A.M., but he tried anyway. Armed with a heavy leather ball, President Hoover began playing just four days after he entered office. Soon 16 players showed up. Two years later, William Atherton Du Puy, a *New York Times* reporter, nicknamed the sport "Hoover-ball."

10   The President's game used a six-pound medicine ball. (Injured patients in hospitals often exercised with them to improve muscle strength.) Two teams, with three players each, stood on either side of an eight-foot-high net. Players had to catch the ball tossed by a member of the opposing team and return it over the net without letting it drop on the ground. Passing the ball to a teammate was not allowed. Teams scored points in the same way as a tennis match.

Playing Rain or Shine

11   According to White House records, President Hoover played almost every morning from 7:00 to 7:30. At 7:30, a factory near the Potomac River blew its whistle—the sign for the men to stop the game and begin the workday. The teams, made up of cabinet members and other White House officials, played in snow and rain and even on holidays. Sunday was the only day off. They moved inside a few times, and the President canceled just once to prepare for an important speech.

12   William Du Puy reported that Hoover-ball players "are as noisy ... as they would be at ... recess time in the old schoolyard" and "the President is a vigorous and forceful performer on the Hoover-ball court. His specialty is catching high ones and throwing them in hard-to-get returns."

13   Hoover-ball was indeed good for the President. He dropped 25 pounds and never missed a day of work because of illness.

14   After President Hoover left office in 1933, Hoover-ball disappeared, but 50 years later, small groups in the United States began playing the game. And today, people as far away as Australia play Hoover-ball.

15   President Hoover did more than lead the United States. He helped to invent a new sport and found a different way to stay fit and healthy.

> *"It required less skill than tennis, was faster and more vigorous, and therefore gave more exercise in a short time."*
>
> —President Hoover

Directions: Answer the following questions. If you need more space to write an answer, write your answer on your own paper.

71 Which paragraph is organized by making a claim and then supporting it with details?

   A Paragraph 9

   B Paragraph 10

   C Paragraph 13

   D Paragraph 14

72 What do the words "Rain or Shine" refer to in the title of the last section?

   A how they played early in the morning

   B how they played in any weather

   C how they played every day except Sunday

   D how they played in two teams

73 The first three paragraphs describe the game, but the author does not reveal who is playing or where the game is being played until paragraph 4. Explain why the author presents the information this way. Use details from the article to support your answer.

74 Describe the problem Hoover describes in paragraph 7. How does Hoover solve the problem? Use details from the article to support your answer.

75 What does the quote by President Hoover at the end of the article tell? How does it help readers understand why President Hoover played Hoover-ball? Use details from the article to support your answer.

76 Paragraph 12 includes a quote by the reporter William Du Puy. Describe **two** important details about the game the quote helps readers imagine. Explain why each detail is important to the main ideas of the article.

77 A play on words can involve using a word that has two meanings related to a topic. Which word in the title of the article is a play on words? Describe the **two** meanings related to the topic of the article.

78 Read this sentence from paragraph 3 of the article.

"The distant sound of a factory whistle blows, ending the game."

How does the section "Playing Rain or Shine" give additional information on what is described in this sentence? Use details from the article to support your answer.

79 What details included in the article show that the author researched the topic? How does the research included make the information seem trustworthy? Use at least **three** examples that show the author's research in your answer.

Planning Space

You can write notes, make a list, or draw a chart to help plan your answer.

_____

_____

_____

_____

_____

_____

_____

_____

_____

_____

_____

_____

80 Reread the first three paragraphs of the article. Explain how these paragraphs show that Hoover-ball is a good fitness activity. What details does the author include to show the fitness benefits? Use details from the article to support your answer.

Planning Space

You can write notes, make a list, or draw a chart to help plan your answer.

_____

_____

_____

_____

_____

_____

_____

_____

_____

_____

_____

_____

Directions: Read the passage. Then answer the questions that follow it.

The Wise Men of Gotham

Adapted from a Play by Augusta Stevenson

SCENE I

TIME: one morning long ago
PLACE: the highroad to Gotham

1   *[Enter HODGE, PODGE, NODGE, and SCRODGE; each carries an ax and each chuckles to himself.]*

2   HODGE: Well, the last tree is down!

3   PODGE: Down and across the road!

4   NODGE: Not a horse can get through them!

5   SCRODGE: How angry it will make the king! He would hang us if he knew we cut the trees and let them fall across the road.

6   PODGE: He will not know. Not a Gotham man would tell him!

7   HODGE: They have not forgotten what havoc his last visit brought upon them.

8   PODGE: Everything he saw and liked, he took.

9   NODGE: And would not pay for it!

10 PODGE *(looking off)*: He is coming now! He is on the hill!

11 SCRODGE: He has his soldiers with him!

12 NODGE: He must not see us! Come!

13 *[They run off. Enter the KING and SOLDIERS.]*

14 KING: Look how the road from here is filled with trees!

15 SOLDIER: Just as it was back there!

16 KING: I know! It was done to keep me out of Gotham! I know! *(He stamps his feet.)* Here, you!

17 SOLDIER *(saluting)*: Yes, your Majesty.

18 KING: Get to Gotham, if you have to crawl. Tell these men of Gotham I shall come again.

19 SOLDIER: Yes, your Majesty.

20 KING: And when I do—and when I do—[*He stops.*]

21 SOLDIER: Yes, your Majesty?

22 KING: And when I do, I'll have their noses! I'll have the Gotham nose of every Gotham man cut off his Gotham face! Go, now, and tell them that!

23 SOLDIER *(saluting)*: Yes, your Majesty.

24 [*He goes.*]

25 KING: We will now return the way we came. *(He shakes his finger toward Gotham.)* I'll have your noses, that I will!

26 [*He goes with his soldiers.*]

SCENE II

TIME: one month later
PLACE: a field near Gotham

27 [*The* OLD MEN, *the* YOUNG MEN, *and the* CHILDREN *are in the field.*]

28 AN OLD MAN: Well, the king's men have taken all the trees away.

29 A YOUNG MAN: A good month's work it made them, too!

30 ANOTHER OLD MAN: And now the king will come again!

31 *[Enter HODGE, PODGE, NODGE, and SCRODGE.]*

32 SCRODGE: The king is coming!

33 CHILDREN: Oh dear! We'll lose our noses!

34 HODGE: Now get you back to Gotham, children! You will not lose your noses.

35 PODGE: Quick, now—before the king comes!

36 *[The children go, holding their noses.]*

37 NODGE: Now, Gotham men, do you all know what to do?

38 OLD MEN: Aye! Aye!

39 YOUNG MEN: Aye! Aye!

40 *[All the men begin to work.]*

41 PODGE: I think this will save our noses.

42 *[Enter the KING and the SOLDIERS.]*

43 KING: Is there a tree left on the road?

44 SOLDIER: We took them all away, Sire.

45 KING: Then go and get our horses. We will ride into this Gotham town. *(The soldier salutes and goes.)* Where do you roll these stones, old men?

46 AN OLD MAN: Uphill to help the sun rise.

47 KING: What! To help the sun rise?

48 OLD MAN: Yes, your Majesty.

49 KING: Don't you know that the sun will rise without help?

50 OLD MAN: Will it? Well, well! Who would have thought of that!

51 KING: You foolish fellows! Well, go on and roll your stones. Now tell me why you grunt, young men?

52 A YOUNG MAN: Oh, we do the grunting while our fathers do the work.

53 KING: Ha, ha! Well, go on and grunt. Now what are you men doing?

54 HODGE: There is a cuckoo here, your Majesty. We are building a wall around it, Sire.

55 KING: Why build a wall around it?

56 NODGE: To keep it from flying away.

57 KING: Ha, ha! Don't you know that the bird can fly over the wall?

58 HODGE: Well, well! Who would have thought of that! How very wise you are, Sire!

59   KING: You foolish fellows! Well, go on and build your wall. *(Enter SCRODGE, carrying a door on his back.)* Where are you going with that door?

60   SCRODGE: I am going on a journey, Sire.

61   KING: Why do you carry a door?

62   SCRODGE: I left my money at home, Sire.

63   KING: Why didn't you leave the door at home?

64   SCRODGE: I was afraid of thieves. If I have the door with me, they can't break it open to get in.

65   KING: You foolish fellow! Why didn't you leave your door at home and carry your money?

66   SCRODGE: Well, well! Who would have thought of that! How very wise you are, Sire!

67   KING: Ha, ha, ha! Well, go on and carry your door. *(To Soldiers.)* These Gotham men are foolish. Does it not seem so to you?

68   SOLDIERS: Aye, Sire!

69   KING: I'll let them keep their noses. They knew no better than to cut down the trees. Come, we will go away and leave them.

70   *[The* KING *and* SOLDIERS *go.]*

71   GOTHAM MEN: Ha, ha, ha!

Directions: Answer the following questions. If you need more space to write an answer, write your answer on your own paper.

81 Read this line from Scene I.

> *"HODGE: They have not forgotten what havoc his last visit brought upon them."*

What does the word *havoc* mean?

A excitement

B joy

C disorder

D sadness

82 In the first scene, what is the main reason the king is angry about the fallen trees?

A He fears he will have to pay to fix the road.

B He believes the men are wasting important timber.

C He thinks the men are trying to keep him away.

D He worries that the trees may harm his horses.

83 Why do you feel the author used the names Hodge, Podge, Nodge, and Scrodge? What do these names suggest about the characters? Use details from the play to support your answer.

84 At the opening of the play, the characters are cutting trees down. How does the author use dialogue to explain why the characters are doing this? Use details from the play to support your answer.

85 The play includes details that describe actions for characters to carry out. Give **two** examples of actions the king carries out in Scene I. Explain what each action shows about the king.

86 How did cutting down the trees in Scene I affect the king? Explain how the setting and the dialogue at the beginning of Scene II show the effect on the king. Use details from the play to support your answer.

87 At the end of Scene I, the king tells his soldier to give a message to the people of Gotham. Do the people of Gotham receive this message? Use details from the play to explain how you can tell.

88 Complete the chart below to summarize the **four** foolish things that the king observes in Scene II.

What the King Observes	Why It Is Foolish

89 Are the main characters really foolish or were they doing foolish things on purpose? Use at least **two** specific details from the play to support your conclusion.

Planning Space

You can write notes, make a list, or draw a chart to help plan your answer.

_____

_____

_____

_____

_____

_____

_____

_____

_____

_____

_____

_____

90 Explain why the king decided to let the people keep their noses. How did the actions of Hodge, Podge, Nodge, and Scrodge lead to this decision? Use details from the play to support your answer.

Planning Space

You can write notes, make a list, or draw a chart to help plan your answer.

_____

_____

_____

_____

_____

_____

_____

_____

_____

_____

_____

_____

Directions: Read the passage. Then answer the questions that follow it.

Living in a Wildlife Camp

By Claire J. Griffin

1   Meet 12-year-old Madison McNutt and 8-year-old Wilder McNutt. These two boys' parents are researchers who study wild dogs in Botswana. A typical day begins with the boys waking up and dressing in their tree house.

6:30 A.M. Eat Breakfast by the Fire

2   Madison and Wilder gather around the campfire with their parents, their teacher, and the other researchers, about 10 people in all. In summer, the weather is hot, but winter mornings can be cold. Peggy, the cook, can make anything over the open fire, even pancakes.

7:30 A.M. Look for Animal Tracks

3   The boys help look for animals near camp. They have two ways of doing this.

4   The first way is to look for tracks in the sand. Honey badgers, hyenas, or leopards might have visited camp in the night.

5   The second way of finding an animal is by radio. The researchers have fitted some wild animals with collars that give off radio signals. A tower near camp picks up the signals. Most of the animals (lions, wild dogs, and others) live in groups. If the researchers find one animal, they usually have found the whole group.

8:00 A.M. Read, Write, Dissect a Leopard

6   On weekday mornings, Madison and Wilder have classes. Usually, the boys do typical schoolwork. But sometimes they may take on something special, such as helping to dissect a leopard that died near camp.

7   Wilder says, "I liked the paws best. The pads were soft, but the claws were sharp. The paws were flexible, and if you squeezed them, you could make the toes move. It was kind of gross but also very cool."

8   Saturday or Sunday morning can mean a game drive, which is a trip in the open-topped Land Rover to observe wildlife. As long as the McNutts stay in the vehicle, they are safe, even from lions and leopards. No one knows why the animals don't attack. Maybe predators think humans are part of the Land Rover.

9   The boys and their parents often spot lions, leopards, cheetahs, hyenas, and wild dogs. They also see the animals that these predators eat—zebras, impalas, kudus, and warthogs.

10 Madison describes seeing a cheetah feeding with her two cubs. "We'd never seen cheetahs on a kill so close to the road and so easy to watch," he says. "The mother had killed a young impala. They were totally calm and didn't mind us watching."

12:45 P.M. Stop for Lunch

11 Peggy has made lasagna and fresh-baked bread. Delicious!

1:30 P.M. Have Fun, Play Games

12   In the afternoon, the boys enjoy some free time. They read, play Ping-Pong, or hang out with one of the camp visitors, such as a dwarf mongoose. They also make things. Madison recently surprised Peggy with a new dinner bell. Wilder likes to work on cars. Last year they helped build their tree house.

4:30 P.M. Search for More Wildlife

13   The boys like the Gomoti River at sunset, when the animals come to drink. As the sky turns rosy, elephants stand at the water's edge and snake their trunks into the water. One of them might raise its trunk and shower water over its giant head. The giraffes amble up and spread their stiff legs out to the sides so they can lower their heads and drink. Hundreds of water birds circle overhead. They call loudly and land on the water in a rush of beating wings.

6:30 P.M. Drive Home

14   Night has fallen by the time the family returns to camp. Sometimes their dad lets Madison drive the Land Rover.

7:00 P.M. Eat by the Fire

15   The evening meal might be spaghetti, pizza, chicken, or traditional Botswana food such as *seswaa* (beef stew) and *pap* (cornmeal mush, which they eat with their hands). Afterward, everyone sits around the fire and talks about the day.

8:30 P.M. Hit the Shower

16   The shower is outside, under a tree, behind reed walls. The water comes from a metal tank with a wood fire underneath. The water takes hours to get hot, but showering feels good after a long, dusty day.

9:00 P.M. Listen to Night Sounds

17   Wilder and Madison lie in their beds in the tree house, listening to the African night. They may hear the deep cough of a lion or the whoop of a hyena or the worried call of a wild dog that's separated from its pack. The brothers fall asleep under the star-filled African sky and dream of tomorrow's adventures.

Directions: Answer the following questions. If you need more space to write an answer, write your answer on your own paper.

91 Which meaning of the word *game* is used in paragraph 8?

A willing and ready

B brave and determined

C a type of pastime

D wild animals

92 The details in the last paragraph are used to suggest that the boys find living in the wildlife camp

A frightening

B boring

C challenging

D interesting

93 Describe the structure of the section titled "Look for Animal Tracks." How do the three paragraphs fit together? Use details from the article to support your answer.

94 One of the sections is titled "Read, Write, Dissect a Leopard." How does this title surprise the reader? What does the title suggest about how the boys' school day compares with typical school days? Use details from the article to support your answer.

95 What new information does Wilder's firsthand account in paragraph 7 give? What does his account suggest about how Wilder feels about his life? Use details from the article to support your answer.

96 Closely reread paragraph 13. The author chooses words to create a clear image of how each animal moves. Complete the chart by identifying the phrase that best shows how each animal moves. Describe what each phrase tells you about how the animal moves.

Animal	Language Used to Describe the Animal's Movement	What the Language Tells About How the Animal Moves
elephants		
giraffes		
water birds		

97 Why is fire important in the wildlife camp? Use at least **two** specific examples of how fire is used to support your answer.

98 Describe the structure of the whole article. How does the structure support the article's main purpose? Use details from the article to support your answer.

99 The section "Read, Write, Dissect a Leopard" includes quotes from both Wilder and Madison. In what main way does Madison sound different from Wilder? How do these quotes help show their different ages? Use details from the article to support your answer.

Planning Space

You can write notes, make a list, or draw a chart to help plan your answer.

100 The article is based around a day in the life of Madison and Wilder. How can you tell that the article does not describe one specific day? Explain why the author did not describe just one specific day. Use details from the article to support your answer.

Planning Space

You can write notes, make a list, or draw a chart to help plan your answer.

Directions: Read the following two passages. Then answer the questions that follow.

I Love the World

By Eileen Spinelli

1   I love the world when it is white,
     when snowflakes fall in winter light
     to cover everything in sight.

2   I love the world when it is blue—
     a sweeping, rented beach-house view:
     blue sea, blue sky, blue dolphins, too.

3   I love the world when it is green,
     with fields of corn and climbing bean
     and rows of peppers in between.

4   I love the world when it is red,
     when scarlet leaves make mice a bed
     and sunset crimsons overhead.

5   Each season's grace and gifts are mine—
     the purple hills, the silver vine. . . .
     And so, dear world,
     this valentine.

I Like It When It's Mizzly

By Aileen Fisher

1   I like it when it's mizzly
    and just a little drizzly
    so everything looks far away
    and make-believe and frizzly.

2   I like it when it's foggy
    and sounding very froggy.
    I even like it when it rains
    on streets and weepy windowpanes
    and catkins in the poplar tree
    and *me*.

Directions: Use "I Love the World" to answer the following questions. If you need **more space** to write an answer, write your answer on your own paper.

101 How does the first-person point of view most affect the poem?

    A It allows the reader to form his or her own opinion.

    B It allows the reader to imagine the scenes described.

    C It allows the speaker to describe her feelings.

    D It allows the speaker to compare the seasons.

102 In the second stanza, the word *sweeping* is used to show that the view is

    A beautiful

    B wide

    C bright

    D clean

103 Which line from the poem creates the clearest image of the color of something?

    A "when snowflakes fall in winter light"

    B "and rows of peppers in between."

    C "and sunset crimsons overhead."

    D "Each season's grace and gifts are mine—"

104 Explain what the speaker means by "this valentine" in the last stanza. How is the poem like a valentine? Use details from the poem to support your answer.

105 The ideas in the poem are divided by topic. Explain how the rhyme pattern and the stanzas work together to achieve this.

106 The first four stanzas all begin by describing a color. Complete the chart below by listing the color and the season it represents. Then list **one** image described that represents the season.

Color	Season	Image

Directions: Use "I Like It When It's Mizzly" to answer the following questions. If you need more space to write an answer, write your answer on your own paper.

107 The poem includes some made-up words. What does the use of these words suggest about the age of the speaker? Use **two** specific examples of made-up words to support your answer.

108 The poem describes "weepy windowpanes." How does the word *weepy* help the reader imagine the raindrops? Use details from the poem to support your answer.

109 Does the rhythm of the poem suggest a calm or an excited feeling? Use details from the poem to support your conclusion.

Directions: Use both "I Love the World" and "I Like It When It's Mizzly" to answer the following question.

110 In both poems, the speaker describes how she feels about nature. Think about the ideas in each poem, the details included, and the techniques used. Write an essay comparing how each speaker presents her view. Include at least **two** similarities and **two** differences in your essay. Use information from both poems to support your answer.

Planning Space
You can complete the chart below to help plan your answer.

	I Love the World	I Like It When It's Mizzly
Ideas		
Details		
Techniques		

_____

_____

_____

_____

_____

_____

_____

_____

_____

_____

_____

_____

_____

_____

_____

_____

_____

_____

_____

_____

_____

_____

_____

_____

_____

Directions: Read the following two passages. Then answer the questions that follow.

The Dolphin Who Loved Games

By Lyle Berg

1   Years ago, I studied biology—the science of living things. I was fascinated by dolphins. When I had the chance to work with scientists who studied how dolphins lived, swam, and talked to one another, I took it.

2   One day, a dolphin named Peg was brought to our facility and placed in what we called the Big Tank. It was a round pool of filtered salt water, about 60 feet across and 5 feet deep. Six other friendly dolphins lived in the Big Tank, but Peg seemed especially friendly. Whenever I was working around the tank, she would swim along the side, staying as close to me as she could.

Peg's Toy Ball

3   I wondered if she would like something to play with, so I went to a store and bought a yellow ball about the size of a soccer ball. The next morning, I tossed the ball into her pool. As soon as she saw it, she shot through the water and tucked the ball under her left pectoral fin—one of the two fins that dolphins have in front.

4   From that day on, she always had that yellow ball with her, and she always tucked it under the same fin. When I walked up to the tank, she would swim over, let the ball go, and use her long snout to flip it up for me to catch.

Race to the Ball

5   Peg loved that game, but there was another one she liked even better. My dog liked to play a game in which I would throw a ball and we would race each other to get it. The dog was much

faster and always got there first. I wanted to try this game with Peg, too.

6   The next time she tossed me the ball, I threw it to the far edge of her pool. Then I started to run around the edge of the pool as fast as I could.

7   She liked the game, but she played it differently than my dog did. Instead of going fast, she swam slowly across the pool, getting to the ball just before I did. Peg should have been able to get to her ball way ahead of me. She only had to swim across her tank and could hit speeds of up to 20 miles per hour. But I had to run all the way around the edge in my clumsy rubber boots. I wasn't nearly as fast.

8   I wondered, "Why didn't she swim faster? Was it more fun getting to the ball at the last second and swooshing it away just before I picked it up?"

9   But that wasn't all that was different. Peg didn't always get to the ball first. Once in a while, she let me get to the ball first. I

wondered why. The only thing I could think of was that she didn't want me to get discouraged and stop playing with her.

Playing with Gulls

10 Peg made up another game all by herself.

11 At feeding time, Peg would often save bits of fish and use them to play with the gulls hanging around the pool.

12 A few gulls always sat on the edge, hoping to pick up scraps of fish. The gulls stayed on the edge because if they landed in the water, the dolphins swam under them and tossed them into the air. (Today, gulls are kept away from dolphins in marine mammal facilities to protect the dolphins from a sick gull that might make them sick.)

13 To play her "Gull Game," Peg took a piece of fish in her teeth and, with a flick of her head, tossed it into the water, near one of the gulls. The gull would quickly lean out over the edge and reach down to get the food.

14 If the food landed too close to the gull, Peg shot over and grabbed the fish in her teeth before the gull could grab it. Then Peg backed up and tried again. If she got the distance just right, the gull would reach too far, lose its balance, and fall into the water with a *plop*. Peg always let the gull keep the fish and didn't toss the bird up in the air, but she did *chitter-chatter*. I supposed she was laughing. I know I was.

15 During my work at the facility, I never learned to speak "dolphin." But Peg and I had a lot of fun playing together, and the two of us seemed to communicate just fine.

Animals and Their Trainers: A Good Team

By Sara F. Shacter

1   Ever wish you could speak to a sparrow, chat with a cheetah, or babble to a baboon? Then think about becoming an animal trainer. Brett Smith is a trainer at Chicago's Lincoln Park Zoo. He says training animals is almost like talking to them.

2   In a zoo or aquarium, an animal and its trainer are a team. Trainers learn to read their animals' behavior to figure out what each animal wants and needs. Animals learn to cooperate with their teachers. This teamwork makes it possible for each animal to live comfortably and get the best care.

3   For everyone's safety, trainers need to teach animals how to behave during a checkup. Do visits to the doctor's office make you squirm? Imagine trying to examine a squirming, trumpeting elephant! Elephants learn how to place their feet so veterinarians can check them. Dolphins learn how to place their tails so veterinarians can take blood samples.

4   At some aquariums, dolphins are taught how to protect themselves from humans' mistakes. Sometimes people drop things into the dolphins' tank. In the water, a plastic bag looks a lot like a squid. But a dolphin could die if it eats the bag. So these dolphins are trained to bring stray objects to the trainers.

5 Because trainers and their animals spend so much time together, their bond of trust is strong. This bond helps trainers do important research. For example, a trainer might be able to get up close when a mother is feeding her new baby. That's something most wild animals wouldn't allow.

Fun and Rewards

6 How do trainers teach animals? Ken Ramirez is the head trainer at Chicago's John G. Shedd Aquarium. He says that animals and people learn best the same way: through fun and rewards.

7 Mr. Ramirez doesn't punish. He wants the animals to have a good time. When the animal does what it's supposed to do, it gets a reward. Often the reward is food, but it can be something else. Belugas (white whales), for example, love having their tongues tickled.

8   Trainers believe that it's also important to give animals the chance to play. New sights, sounds, and experiences keep animals' minds and bodies healthy. At the Shedd aquarium, dolphins enjoy watching their reflections in mirrors. One dolphin looks at herself for hours. At the Lincoln Park Zoo, lions play with piñatas. The lions rush up, smack their prey, and jump away. Once they're sure the piñatas won't fight back, the lions rip them open. They find the food or bone inside and make shredded paper their new toy.

9   Training animals takes time and patience, but the rewards are huge. Ken Ramirez says a trainer is an animal's "parent, doctor, playmate, and best friend." Animals may not speak our language, but they have much to tell us.

Who's Training Whom?

10   Ken Ramirez once worked with a dolphin that could always find a piece of trash in his tank, even when the pool looked clean. The dolphin earned a fish reward for each piece of trash he turned in.

11   Soon the trainers became suspicious. They began saving everything the dolphin found, from bags to newspaper scraps. When they noticed that the newspaper scraps fit together, they realized what was going on.

12   The dolphin had found a little nook in the tank, perfect for storing trash. When he wanted a snack, he'd grab some garbage and turn it in for a treat.

Directions: Use "The Dolphin Who Loved Games" to answer the following questions. If you need more space to write an answer, write your answer on your own paper.

111 Which phrase from the article uses language to show fast movement?

   A "swim along the side"

   B "tossed the ball"

   C "shot through the water"

   D "tucked the ball under"

112 Which sentence from "Race to the Ball" is a comparison?

   A "My dog liked to play a game in which I would throw a ball and we would race each other to get it."

   B "The next time she tossed me the ball, I threw it to the far edge of her pool."

   C "She liked the game, but she played it differently than my dog did."

   D "She only had to swim across her tank and could hit speeds of up to 20 miles per hour."

113 Based on the information in "Peg's Toy Ball," what part of a dolphin is a *snout*?

   A fin

   B flipper

   C tail

   D nose

114 How does the author's description of the "Gull Game" make it seem amusing? Describe at least **two** ways the author emphasizes the humor of the game.

115 In the section "Race to the Ball," the author makes assumptions about why Peg does things. Describe **two** assumptions the author makes. Explain how you know that they are assumptions.

Directions: Use "Animals and Their Trainers: A Good Team" to answer the following questions. If you need more space to write an answer, write your answer on your own paper.

116 Read paragraph 2 of the article. Explain what the word *cooperate* means. Describe **two** details in the paragraph that help show the meaning of the word.

117 The article describes the purpose of training dolphins. Complete the graphic organizer below by listing **two** examples of problems and explaining how training the dolphin solves the problem.

Problem		Solution
	→	

Problem		Solution
	→	

118 "Who's Training Whom?" is the title of the last section of the article. What does this title imply? Explain how it relates to the events described in the section. Use details from the section to support your answer.

119 Ken Ramirez states that animals are best trained using both fun and rewards. How is the training of the lions at Lincoln Park Zoo an example of using fun and rewards? Use details from the article to support your answer.

Directions: Use "The Dolphin Who Loved Games" and "Animals and Their Trainers: A Good Team" to answer the following question.

120 Both articles describe how people work with and train dolphins. Compare the point of view of the two articles. Which point of view best shows the relationship that forms between dolphins and the people they work with? Which point of view best shows the purpose of forming these relationships? Use information from both articles to support your answer.

Planning Space

You can complete the chart below to help plan your answer.

	The Dolphin Who Loved Games	Animals and Their Trainers: A Good Team
What is the point of view?		
Does the point of view show the relationship between dolphins and people?		
Does the point of view show the purpose of forming the relationship?		

_____

_____

_____

_____

_____

_____

_____

_____

_____

_____

_____

Part C:

Integration of Knowledge and Ideas

Literary, Informational, and Paired Passages with Multiple Choice, Short Response, Extended Response, and Essay Questions

Common Core State Standards for Informational Text (Grade 4)

RI.4.7　Interpret information presented visually, orally, or quantitatively (e.g., in charts, graphs, diagrams, time lines, animations, or interactive elements on Web pages) and explain how the information contributes to an understanding of the text in which it appears.

RI.4.8　Explain how an author uses reasons and evidence to support particular points in a text.

RI.4.9　Integrate information from two texts on the same topic in order to write or speak about the subject knowledgeably.

Common Core State Standards for Literary Text (Grade 4)

RL.4.7　Make connections between the text of a story or drama and a visual or oral presentation of the text, identifying where each version reflects specific descriptions and directions in the text.

RL.4.8　(Not applicable to literature)

RL.4.9　Compare and contrast the treatment of similar themes and topics (e.g., opposition of good and evil) and patterns of events (e.g., the quest) in stories, myths, and traditional literature from different cultures.

Directions: Read the passage. Then answer the questions that follow it.

2,000-Year-Old Homework!

Unroll a wad of paper and discover the secrets of ancient Egypt.

By Joli Allen

1   Dr. Todd Hickey opens a rusted tin box filled to the brim with tattered pieces of 2,000-year-old paper from Egypt. Dr. Hickey, a papyrologist (pap-eh-ROL-ah-jist), is excited about this rare type of treasure. It isn't covered in gold, but it is indeed priceless. That's because those tattered pieces of paper are papyrus. Papyrus tells us much about the secrets of life in ancient Egypt.

2   The Egyptians made this paper from papyrus plants that grew near the Nile River. Before papyrus, Egyptians mostly used copper chisels to carve words called hieroglyphs into stone. Papyrus made writing easier.

Writing to Go

3   With papyrus, Egyptians could now write signs and symbols using brushes, reed pens, and ink made from soot scraped out of cooking vessels and oil lamps. And they could take their writing wherever they went.

4   Dr. Hickey has already studied hundreds of the papyri. Some contain spells that the Egyptians wrote down and carried with them. They believed spells gave them magical protection or

power. Other papyri give directions for making powerful medicine. Archaeologists even found 2,000-year-old homework. A schoolboy had copied his lesson over and over with a reed quill.

From Trash to Treasure

5   When papyri weren't needed anymore for writing, they were tossed in the trash. The Egyptians reused these unwanted papyri to make papier-mâché. They shaped masks for human mummies or used the papyri to wrap animal mummies.

6   "Think of it as the ancient Egyptians' form of recycling," says Dr. Hickey.

7   Dr. Hickey needs to uncover valuable writings in the waste paper. And that is no easy task. It can take days to unroll just one wad of paper. First it is dampened to help it soften and relax. Then the paper is unrolled a bit. Dirt and gunk are carefully scraped off. The papyrologists must be careful not to scrape away the ink or paint underneath the dirt. The paper is unrolled a bit more. When the papyrus is completely unrolled, papyrologists look for torn pieces that fit together.

8   After the pieces are joined, is the job finished? No. The secrets from the past are still hidden, because words are missing from the worn bits of papyrus. The handwriting is faded and in ancient languages.

It's All Greek to Me

9   When Dr. Hickey decodes papyri, he needs to know other languages besides Egyptian. Ancient Egypt was ruled by the Greeks and Romans at different times, so he has to read and think in Greek and Latin.

10   Once he figures out what a sentence means, he tries to guess what the missing words or letters are in the holes of the papyrus.

11   "It's a challenge, but it is not impossible for papyrologists," Dr. Hickey says. "H—e would lead me to think 'horse' in some contexts, 'house' in others."

12   History leaps to life from each repaired papyrus. Dr. Hickey and other papyrologists found a police report to a royal scribe about a missing person. It reads: "On the 5th of the present month when patrolling the fields near the village ... I learn from the villagers that Theodotos son of Dositheos, having set out in that direction, has not yet returned. I make this report." The reporter also says that he found clues, but not the missing person.

13   Another piece of papyrus gave the dinner menu for a town's sacred crocodiles. The crocodiles were to be served meat, wine, and honey.

14   Some papyri give archaeologists a good idea of what Egyptians read for fun. They enjoyed adventure stories, poetry, plays, and myths.

15   It will take years for Dr. Hickey to study all the papyri in the tin box. He picks up a completed papyrus covered in protective glass. The writing on the papyrus forms a triangle, and the words can be read in several directions. It says the Greek nonsense phrase for a magical spell—similar to *abracadabra*. Too bad it can't be used to make all the papyrus bits in the tin box fall together instantly. But we can look forward to learning more about Egyptian life as each piece is connected.

Directions: Answer the following questions. If you need more space to write an answer, write your answer on your own paper.

121 Read this sentence from paragraph 1.

"It isn't covered in gold, but it is indeed priceless."

What is the main reason the author describes the papyrus as "priceless"?

A It is a form of trash.

B It contains valuable information.

C It is difficult to find.

D It dates back thousands of years.

122 Which sentence in the first section is most important to the main idea of the article?

A "Papyrus tells us much about the secrets of life in ancient Egypt."

B "The Egyptians made this paper from papyrus plants that grew near the Nile River."

C "Before papyrus, Egyptians mostly used copper chisels to carve words called hieroglyphs into stone."

D "Papyrus made writing easier."

123 How did using papyrus instead of stone make writing easier for the Egyptians? Use **two** details from the article to support your answer.

124 The article explains that it can "take days to unroll just one wad of paper." Complete the chart below to show the steps taken to unroll a wad of paper.

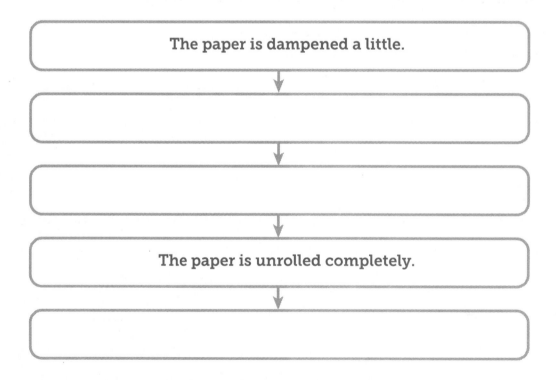

The paper is dampened a little.

↓

↓

↓

The paper is unrolled completely.

↓

125 How does the photograph of the papyrus help show the difficult work that Dr. Hickey does? Use details from the article to support your answer.

126 The author includes illustrations to represent things that were learned about how the Egyptians lived. Choose **three** illustrations from the article. Describe what the illustration shows and what finding about Egyptian life it represents.

Description of the Illustration	The Finding About Egyptian Life Represented

127 Do you feel that the illustrations in the article make the papyrus findings seem important or unimportant? Use information from the article to support your conclusion.

128 Explain why Dr. Hickey needs to know Egyptian, Greek, and Latin. Use at least **two** details from the article to support your answer.

129 The papyrus contains valuable information, but it is not easy to obtain the information. Describe at least **two** challenges that make analyzing the papyrus difficult. Explain how each challenge can be overcome. Use information from the article to support your answer.

Planning Space

You can complete the chart below to help plan your answer.

Challenges that Make Analyzing the Papyrus Difficult	How the Challenge Is Overcome

_____

_____

_____

_____

_____

_____

_____

_____

_____

_____

_____

_____

130 Scientists like Dr. Todd Hickey study papyrus to learn about life in ancient Egypt. Explain why Dr. Hickey studies papyrus. Give **three** examples of things that Dr. Hickey has learned by studying papyrus. Use information from the article to support your answer.

Planning Space

You can write notes, make a list, or draw a chart to help plan your answer.

Directions: Read the passage. Then answer the questions that follow it.

Double Trouble

By Sheila C. Bair

I only needed $10. Would my sister lend me the money?

1   When I was eight, I wanted a Super Sleuth Utility Belt more than anything else in the world. It had a see-in-the-dark collapsible telescope. It also had an invisible-ink pen, a voice scrambler, a fingerprint kit, a magnifying glass, and a decoder—all attached to a shiny black plastic belt. I just *had* to have one.

2   I needed $10 to buy it, but, as usual, I was broke. I decided to ask my 11-year-old sister, Kathleen, for a loan. (She always had money.) I went to her room, fell to my knees, and begged her for the cash. Laughing, she agreed to lend me the money, but then she said, "I'm going to charge you 10 percent compound interest every month until you pay me back."

3   "Compound interest—what's that?" I asked.

4   "Well, *interest* is what you call the extra money borrowers have to pay back on a loan," she explained. "*Compound interest* means that the interest payments get bigger and bigger the longer you take to pay back the loan."

5   She pulled a pencil and tablet out of her dresser and settled down next to me on her bed.

6   "Look. I'm going to charge you 10 percent interest on the amount you owe me every month." She scribbled on her tablet. "Figuring 10 percent of $10 is easy. Just move the decimal over one place to the left.

7 10% of $10.00 = $1.00

8 "Now, add that to the $10 I'm lending you. To repay the loan, you will need to give me $11 after one month."

9 $10 + $1.00 = $11.00

10 "OK," I said. That seemed simple enough.

11 "If you wait two months to pay me back, your debt will grow from $10 to $11. So I'll be charging you interest on $11.

12 10% of $11.00 = $1.10

13 "Then I will add that interest to the $11 you already owe me, for a total of $12.10. That's what you'll owe after two months."

14 "Sure. I get it," I said, though truthfully, I was getting confused.

15 "I want to make sure you *do* get it, Sheila," she said, pointing at her tablet. "After three months, it's going to get worse. I will be charging you 10 percent interest on $12.10.

16 10% of $12.10 = $1.21

17 "Then I will add that interest to the $12.10 you already owe me, for a total of $13.31."

18 $12.10 + $1.21 = $13.31

19 "All right, already!" I said. "Look, my birthday is in a month, and I always get money for my birthday. I'll pay you back $11 in a month. OK?"

20 "I hope you do," said my sister.

21 Kathleen lent me the money, and I bought the utility belt. My birthday came a month later. Sure enough, my Grandma Bair

gave me $10 and my Grandma Brenneman gave me $5. Unfortunately, that $15 was just the amount I needed to buy a Super Sleuth Lie Detector Kit with fingertip sensors to go with my utility belt.

22 I put off paying my sister for a month. After another month, I forgot about the loan.

23 Several months later, on Christmas morning, my sister and I were rooting around in our Christmas stockings to see what Santa had left us. We each found a $20 bill stuffed in the toes.

24 I was just tucking the crisp green bill into my pajama pocket when Kathleen tapped me on the shoulder.

25 "Sorry, kiddo. That's mine. I'm collecting on your debt."

26 "Huh?" I said. Then I remembered the loan. "Hey! How can it be that much? I only borrowed $10."

27 "True," she said, "but interest has been compounding for eight months. Now you owe me $21.43." She paused, then added, "You can pay me the $1.43 out of your next allowance."

28 I refused to believe that a $10 loan could more than double so quickly. Much to my annoyance, my sister got her pencil and tablet again, and showed me exactly how it all added up.

29 My head hurt as I tried to keep track of Kathleen's calculations, but *this* time, I got the basic idea. When interest is compounded, the interest payments get bigger and bigger the longer you wait to pay back the loan. I learned the hard way that borrowing money can be "double trouble" in no time at all.

How My $10 Loan More Than Doubled in Eight Months

30 Here is the chart Kathleen gave me that showed how she calculated my debt.

Month	Debt Amount +	10% Interest = (rounded)	New Debt
May	$10.00	$1.00	$11.00
June	$11.00	$1.10	$12.10
July	$12.10	$1.21	$13.31
August	$13.31	$1.33	$14.64
September	$14.64	$1.46	$16.10
October	$16.10	$1.61	$17.71
November	$17.71	$1.77	$19.48
December	$19.48	$1.95	**$21.43!**

31 As my debt grew larger and larger, the interest payments grew larger and larger. In fact, if I had waited 10 years to pay my sister back, I would have owed her $927,090.69—almost a million dollars! Good thing she didn't wait that long to remind me.

Directions: Answer the following questions. If you need more space to write an answer, write your answer on your own paper.

131 What is the main purpose of paragraph 29?

   A to show that Sheila's math skills have improved

   B to show that Sheila has learned a lesson

   C to suggest that Sheila should be more sensible

   D to suggest that Sheila needs to save more money

132 Which statement best summarizes a main theme of the story?

   A Look before you leap.

   B Always follow your heart.

   C Better late than never.

   D Two wrongs don't make a right.

133 Compare the illustrations of the two girls. Which illustration shows Sheila and which one shows Kathleen? Explain how you can tell.

134 Reread paragraph 4 of the story. What does what Kathleen says show the reader about her understanding of money? Use details from the story to support your answer.

135 The author includes calculations in paragraphs 6 through 18. Explain what these calculations show and why they are important. Use details from the story to support your answer.

136 Give **two** specific examples of where Kathleen tries to warn Sheila about the importance of understanding compound interest. Explain how these examples foreshadow the ending of the story.

137 The title of the story is "Double Trouble." Describe **two** ways the title relates to the theme of the story.

138 Read these sentences from the beginning of the story.

> *"I only needed $10. Would my sister lend me the money?"*

Do these sentences describe Sheila's main problem in the story? Use details from the story to support your conclusion.

139 The section "How My $10 Loan More Than Doubled in Eight Months" explains how the amount owed increased. Describe **three** ways the information in this section emphasizes the power of compound interest. Use specific examples from the section in your answer.

Planning Space

You can write notes, make a list, or draw a chart to help plan your answer.

140 The story tells about a girl who learns an important lesson. What lesson does Sheila learn? What would she most likely do the next time she does not have enough money for something? Use details from the story to support your answer.

Planning Space

You can write notes, make a list, or draw a chart to help plan your answer.

_____

_____

_____

_____

_____

_____

_____

_____

_____

_____

_____

_____

_____

_____

Directions: Read the passage. Then answer the questions that follow it.

Learning from a Baby Bear

By Nancy Marie Brown

1   One March day, deep in the woods, I picked up a bear cub and cuddled it. Its little claws looked sharp, but they didn't hurt. Hungry, the cub nuzzled my neck, hoping for milk.

2   Its eyes were pale blue. Surprised and bemused, it looked around at the crowd of people. Its fur was night-black except inside its ears, where it paled to tawny brown. The cub wriggled under my coat and snuggled into my sweater. It mewled softly, and I petted it as if it were just a big kitten.

3   I would never have picked up a bear cub if it hadn't been for Gary Alt. Gary is a wildlife biologist. He had given the mother bear a drug to make her sleep so that he could give her a checkup, as he did every year. While he and his team of scientists worked, he needed people to keep the cubs from wandering off. I had volunteered to help.

Searching for Bears

4   Gary's bears were wild, but they wore collars. Each collar held a radio transmitter that gave out a beep that was silent to the bear, but Gary could hear it with a radio receiver and a big antenna. He would drive along back roads with the antenna sticking out the window of his truck.

5   He tried to find the bears in their winter dens, before they woke up and went wandering. Some denned in caves or rocky clefts. But he'd found one mother bear and her cubs in a culvert under a highway, and another under the porch of a house. (The family hadn't known a bear was living with them.)

6   The day I went with Gary, the first bear he found was in a swamp. We went down steep hills, past gray rocks covered with pale-green lichens. The thick, twisty stems of rhododendron bushes with their waxy, evergreen leaves made it hard to see far. The swamp was frozen over, but the ice was thin. Everyone broke through at least once. We were all wet to the knees.

7   Now and then, Gary would hop onto a rock and hold high the antenna, then slightly change course. But this bear had hidden where we couldn't reach her.

8   The wind had turned cold when we went to find another bear. We followed a narrow trail and crossed a stream on wobbly rocks. (I fell in and got wet feet again.) We stopped in a little brushy clearing surrounded by pines. This second bear, Gary said, was just ahead, over a little knoll. He traded the antenna for a long metal pole with a needle on the end, and went on alone.

9   Patches of snow lay under the trees. I stood on an old barkless log and listened. Wind blew through the pines. Nylon jackets squeaked as the rest of our group came out of the thicket. A twig snapped.

10   Soon Gary was back, grinning. "I don't think she saw me," he said. "I came in from the back side, through the thick stuff. I got within six feet of her, and she never moved." The needle full of

sleeping drug did not seem to bother her. "She never even picked her head up," he said.

11 Finally, I had a chance to hold the cub. The mother bear's den was more like a nest, a comfy hole in a clump of bushes. Her four cubs slept under her paws. Gary lifted a paw and gently picked up a cub by the scruff of its neck. He passed it to me.

12 By checking on bears in their dens every year, Gary and other scientists are learning how far bears roam and what kinds of places they like to call home. They're learning how long bears live and how many cubs are born each year. They're learning how fast the little blue-eyed cub under my coat will grow into a four-hundred-pound bear. And they're learning how much woods we'll need to leave so that the bear can find enough food—without raiding garbage cans.

A Healthy Cub

13 Part of being a healthy mother bear is having healthy cubs, so the scientists gave the cubs checkups, too. Bear cubs are born while the mother is asleep in her den, then they stay close to her warmth. If she wasn't able to find enough food to eat in the summer before, her cubs would be small and sickly.

14 Too soon, someone came for my cub. He weighed five pounds—a good size. When the scientists finished taking measurements, they put metal tags in the cub's ears to identify him the next time. He shook his head, annoyed by his new earrings.

15 As I lifted him off the scientist's lap, the cub squirmed and mewled and was a true nuisance. I was afraid he would wriggle free. Then suddenly, he yawned. I slipped him under my coat, and he clung to my sweater, mewled again, and closed his eyes. Before long, Gary came to set him back under his sleeping mother's paw.

Directions: Answer the following questions. If you need more space to write an answer, write your answer on your own paper.

141 How did the author cuddling the baby bear help scientists?

  A It helped the bear get used to being around people.

  B It allowed the scientists to put the metal tags in the bear's ears.

  C It kept the baby bear from running away.

  D It stopped the mother of the bear from getting upset.

142 According to the graph, at what age are bears smaller than human babies the same age?

  A Newborn

  B First year

  C 2 years

  D 3 years

143 Complete the table below by sorting the places where Gary Alt has found bear dens into usual places and unusual places.

Places Where Bears Den

Usual Places	Unusual Places
1)	1)
2)	2)

144 Reread paragraph 10 of the article. What do the quotes from Gary suggest about how he feels about the work he does? Use details from the article to support your answer.

145 In the first two paragraphs, the author describes holding the bear. How does the author's description emphasize that the bear is harmless? Give at least **two** specific examples to support your answer.

146 How do the collars help scientists track the bears? Why is tracking the bears difficult even with the collars? Use details from the article to support your answer.

147 What is the most likely reason the scientists gave the mother bear a drug but not the baby bear? Use details from the article to support your conclusion.

148 The graph is included to compare humans and bears. Identify the main difference shown and explain how the graph illustrates the difference.

149 The article describes a day the author spent working with Gary Alt. Describe at least **two** things that the author probably found hard about the day. Explain whether or not you feel the difficulties were worth it. Use details from the article to support your answer.

Planning Space

You can write notes, make a list, or draw a chart to help plan your answer.

_____

_____

_____

_____

_____

_____

_____

_____

_____

_____

_____

_____

150 Describe the purpose of the research conducted by Gary Alt and his team. How could this research benefit bears? Use details from the article to support your answer.

Planning Space

You can write notes, make a list, or draw a chart to help plan your answer.

_____

_____

_____

_____

_____

_____

_____

_____

_____

_____

_____

_____

Directions: Read the following two passages. Then answer the questions that follow.

Alexander's Astounding World Feat

By Bradford H. Robie

1. "This is amazing," Alexander told his sister, Amy. "The record for eating hard-boiled eggs is 34 eggs in 30 minutes." He was reading *The Astounding Book of World Feats* by Captain Neville Puffer.

2. "That's disgusting," Amy said.

3. "Someone else ate 51 hot dogs in 12 minutes," Alexander continued.

4. Amy shuddered. "Isn't there any *useful* information? Like the record for running a mile?"

5. Alexander flipped through the pages. "Horatio Hopper skipped rope for 34 hours, stopping only once for a milkshake."

6. Amy shook her head.

7. "I'm going to set a world record, too," Alexander announced.

8. Amy laughed. "Which one? Not making your bed for 30 days in a row?"

9. But Alexander was serious about getting into *The Astounding Book of World Feats*. It was just a matter of *how*.

10. "I know!" he said. "I bet I can seesaw longer than anyone."

11. He checked the book and groaned when he read that a girl from Spain had teeter-tottered for 72 hours. What else could he do?

12. Some business cards lay on the kitchen table. Dad had a business card, and so did Mom. Why not collect business cards and assemble the world's largest collection? "That's it!" he said.

13 Alexander wasted no time in getting cards from his parents, the man painting their house, the neighbors, and the woman who delivered the newspaper. By the end of the week, he had 17 business cards.

That's it!

14 "Hardly a world record," said Amy.

15 As Alexander thumbed through the Sunday paper, an idea hit him. He called his uncle Dex, who was a newspaper reporter.

16 "I'll get a short item in the paper tomorrow," Uncle Dex promised. And he did.

BOY WANTS BUSINESS CARDS

17 If Alexander Wells has his way, he'll soon be listed in *The Astounding Book of World Feats* for amassing the world's largest collection of business cards. To help, send *your* card to Alexander at the following address ...

18 The next day, 5 business cards arrived in the mail. And the day after that, 10. Then 35.

19 "Nice," Alexander said as he shuffled the cards in his hands.

20 Other newspapers picked up the story. In a few weeks, sacks of business cards were coming in from all over the state, from all sorts of people: lawyers, plumbers, engineers, musicians, gardeners, accountants.

21 Alexander soon ran out of space in his bedroom to store the cards. Holding a box of them, he knocked on Amy's door. "Can I put some in here?"

22 "No way," Amy said.

23 So he accumulated them in the attic; he gathered them in the garage. In just three months, his collection grew to more than a million!

24 Uncle Dex wrote a follow-up story: "Boy Collects a Million-Plus Business Cards." It included a picture of Alexander surrounded by his collection. Alexander sent this story to *The Astounding Book of World Feats* along with an official entry form.

25 And finally, he received what he'd been hoping for:

> *Dear Alexander,*
>
> *It is my pleasure to notify you of your record for the world's largest collection of business cards. Your accomplishment will appear in the next edition of* The Astounding Book of World Feats. *Also, you will receive a free trip to our annual awards ceremony.*
>
> *Sincerely,*
>
> *Captain Neville Puffer*

26 "I made it!" Alexander shouted. "I'm in the book!"

27 Amy read the letter, shaking her head. Then she patted her brother's back. "Didn't I always say you could do it?"

28 "Alexander," said his dad, "what will you do with all of those cards?"

29 Alexander asked Uncle Dex to write a final story announcing the record and asking people to stop sending cards. But the cards kept coming! The awards ceremony was held in a fancy hotel. Among the people at Alexander's table were Stringbean Sally, the world's tallest woman, and Ear-to-Ear Lear, the man with the world's widest smile. Next to Alexander sat a girl named Emily, who'd built the tallest replica of the Eiffel Tower with Popsicle sticks.

30 "What are you planning to do next?" Alexander asked Emily.

31 "Have you heard of the Leaning Tower of Pisa?"

32 Alexander nodded. "It's in Italy."

33 "I'd like to build a huge one out of playing cards." Emily sighed. "But it will take forever to collect the cards."

34 Alexander grinned. "Have you considered using business cards?"

But it will take forever to collect the cards.

Don't Try This at Home!

35 In real life, *Guinness Book of World Records* eliminated its "collected cards" category after a similar quest led to a huge amount of unwanted mail.

Running Rabbit
A Kumeyaay Folktale

Retold by Jeannie Beck

1   There was once a rabbit who was known to be the fastest rabbit in the world. The elders often spoke of this rabbit whenever a young boy came of age and it was time to test his hunting skills.

2   One small boy, who had heard the tale of this rabbit many times, decided that he would be the one to finally bring him in. As the years passed and the boy came of age, still no one had managed to bag Running Rabbit.

3   The elders cheered the boy on as he carved his first bow and arrow. He was given three days to hunt the rabbit. It was known that this rabbit always stayed in a certain flat area that was at least a mile long. It was here that the boy waited until he saw Running Rabbit.

4   "I have waited for you for a long time, and now you are old and it is time for you to leave this world," the boy said to the rabbit as he drew back his arrow. But by the time the arrow had left the bow, the rabbit had disappeared.

5   "That rabbit doesn't seem to get older, he just gets faster," the boy said to himself.

6   As night fell, the boy returned to camp, hearing the elders cheering his arrival because they had thought for sure that he would be the one to bring in the tricky old rabbit.

7   The boy did not hunt the next day, but instead searched for the strongest, straightest greasewood plant. From this plant he formed the sleekest arrow. Then he found the healthiest, most powerful elderberry tree from which he carved his new bow.

8   The boy decorated his new tools with elegant feathers from the magical flicker bird. Finally he shaped the sharpest, longest arrowhead, creating the least amount of wind resistance. When all was prepared, he fell asleep satisfied.

9   The next morning the boy returned to the flat and waited with complete confidence for Running Rabbit. As he strained his eyes to see through the early morning mist, he spied a streak of dust cutting through the fog. There he was!

10 The boy drew back his bow, and as the arrow left, so did the rabbit, who was showing off his fast running. About a mile away, the boy could see a large dark cloud rising up from the meadow.

11 When he reached the end of the flat, the boy saw a strange thing. There was his arrow, with the flicker feathers flying in the breeze, pinning a rabbit's fur to the ground. But where was Running Rabbit? The boy searched the meadow for hours before finally returning to camp with just the rabbit's soft coat. The elders thought the boy had made rabbit stew before returning home, so no one ever asked.

12 But the truth was, instead of running away from the boy, the rabbit had been showing off, and when he jumped so high and fast he ran into the arrow's path and got skinned. Running Rabbit narrowly escaped with his life, but not before losing his beautiful coat.

13 The naked rabbit was so embarrassed that he had to hide until he grew a new coat, and from then on he was shy like all the other rabbits.

Directions: Use "Alexander's Astounding World Feat" to answer the following questions. If you need more space to write an answer, write your answer on your own paper.

151 What does paragraph 17 of the story represent?

A a flyer Alexander put up

B an advertisement in a newspaper

C a business card Alexander received

D an article from the record book

152 Why does the author include the last paragraph?

A to summarize the information in the story

B to give a warning related to the topic of the story

C to explain that the events described did not really happen

D to encourage readers to choose a different record to break

153 Look closely at the illustration on page 179. Complete the chart below by listing **two** more details in the illustration and explaining what each detail shows.

Detail	What the Detail Shows
The sister has her mouth covered.	She does not take her brother's goal seriously.

154 In paragraph 25, the author includes the letter Alexander received to show he had broken the record. Why do you think the author included the letter instead of just stating that Alexander received it? Use details from the story to support your answer.

155 Explain the meaning of paragraphs 33 and 34. What do they suggest will happen next? Use details from the story to support your answer.

Directions: Use "Running Rabbit" to answer the following questions. If you need more space to write an answer, write your answer on your own paper.

156 Describe **two** ways you can tell that "Running Rabbit" is a folktale. Use specific examples in your answer.

157 One of the themes of the story is about the dangers of showing off. Explain how the folktale communicates this message. Use details from the story to support your answer.

158 The illustration shows the rabbit as very large compared to the boy. Why do you think the rabbit was shown as large? Use details from the story to support your conclusion.

Directions: Use both "Alexander's Astounding World Feat" and "Running Rabbit" to answer the following questions.

159 Both "Alexander's Astounding World Feat" and "Running Rabbit" are made-up stories. Explain which story you found least realistic. Use examples from both stories to support your answer.

Planning Space

You can complete the chart below to help plan your answer.

Features of "Alexander's Astounding World Feat" that Are Not Realistic	Features of "Running Rabbit" that Are Not Realistic

_____

_____

_____

_____

_____

_____

_____

_____

_____

_____

_____

_____

160 Both stories describe a main character who has a goal. Compare the goals of the two characters and how they achieve their goals. Use details from both stories to support your answer.

Planning Space

You can complete the chart below to help plan your answer.

	Alexander	Boy from "Running Rabbit"
What is the goal?		
How hard is the goal to achieve?		
How does the character try to achieve the goal?		
Is the goal achieved?		

_____

_____

_____

_____

_____

_____

_____

_____

_____

_____

_____

_____

_____

_____

Directions: Read the passage. Then answer the questions that follow it.

Flying Circles Around Mercury

By Ken Croswell, Ph.D.

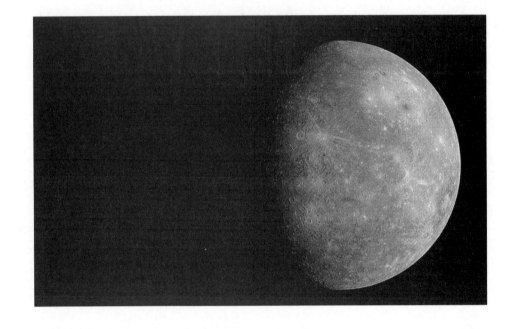

1   Giant craters, steep cliffs, ancient volcanoes, extreme heat and cold: welcome to mysterious Mercury.

2   Mercury is the closest planet to the Sun, and much of it is unexplored.

3   "Mercury is one of the big gaps in our knowledge of the solar system," says Robert Strom at the University of Arizona.

4   In 1974 and 1975, a spacecraft named Mariner 10 flew past Mercury three times and sent back pictures. But the spacecraft showed us only about half the planet.

5   Starting in March 2011, however, a new spacecraft named Messenger will go around the planet again and again and again. It will study Mercury for years and finally send pictures of the whole planet.

Planet of Extremes

6   Mercury is small. It's only 3,032 miles across. That's a bit more than the distance from New York to California.

7   Mercury speeds around the Sun in only 88 days. That's Mercury's year. So if you lived on Mercury, you'd get a birthday every 88 days.

8   But don't move there just yet. Mercury has almost no air to breathe.

9   Plus, you wouldn't like the temperature. As Mercury turns, the side that faces the Sun gets very hot ... and the other side gets very cold. Why? The Sun stays up in Mercury's sky for 88 days, raising the temperature to 800 degrees Fahrenheit (F). That temperature is hot enough to melt lead.

10   After sunset, the night lasts another 88 days, and the temperature plunges to 300 degrees F below zero. That's much colder than Earth's North Pole.

11   Mercury's surface is just as hostile. Like the Moon, it's gray and full of craters. The largest known crater on Mercury is Caloris Basin, which is 960 miles across, wider than Texas. The crater formed when a large asteroid hit the planet.

Mercury and Earth		
	Mercury	**Earth**
Average Distance from Sun	36,000,000 miles	92,960,000 miles
Year	88 days	365¼ days
Full Day (sunrise to sunrise)	176 days	24 hours
Tilt of Axis	0 degrees	23½ degrees
Diameter at Equator	3,032 miles	7,926 miles
Temperature	−300 to +800 F	−129 to +136 F
Number of Moons	0	1

Heart of Iron

12 But on the inside, Mercury differs from the Moon. In fact, it's more like Earth. Both Mercury and Earth have a core of iron.

13 "The very biggest mystery about Mercury is the origin of its large iron core," says Strom.

14 Surrounding the iron core is a rocky mantle and crust. Earth's iron core makes up one-third of Earth's mass. Mercury's iron core is a whopping two-thirds of Mercury's mass.

15 Why is Mercury's iron core so big compared with the rest of the planet? Scientists don't know. But they have some ideas.

16 Maybe, long ago, Mercury had a thicker mantle. Then a huge asteroid hit Mercury and blasted most of the mantle away, leaving the large iron core.

17 Or maybe, long ago, the Sun blazed more brightly. The light might have vaporized most of the rocky mantle.

18 Strom says Messenger will see what Mercury's surface is made of. From that data, scientists hope to deduce the planet's history and see how it got its huge iron core.

19 Motions inside that core generate a magnetic field. So if you took a compass to Mercury, it would work just fine. In contrast, it wouldn't work on Venus, Mars, or the Moon, because they don't have magnetic fields the way Mercury and Earth do.

Ice on Mercury?

20 In 1991, astronomers looked at Mercury's poles and made a surprising discovery. They found what seems to be water in the form of ice.

21 How can ice exist on such a hot planet? The ice probably huddles inside craters that never see sunlight. So the ice doesn't melt. Messenger will tell us whether this ice really exists.

22 On March 18, Messenger is set to go into orbit around Mercury, filling a big gap in our knowledge. Says Strom, "Once we fill that gap, we're going to have a much better understanding of the solar system."

One Discovery: Volcanoes!

The Messenger spacecraft has already made some discoveries, because it flew past the planet twice in 2008 and once in 2009. It has shown us most of the planet's surface.

"In the past, Mercury has been very volcanically active," says planetary scientist Robert Strom. Billions of years ago, these volcanoes erupted and their lava partially covered some of Mercury's craters. However, the volcanoes probably don't erupt today.

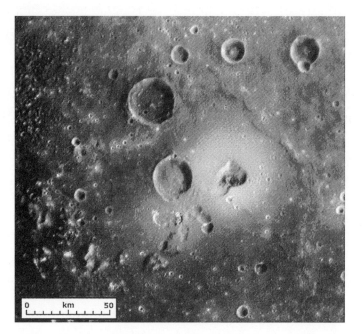

The Messenger spacecraft found this huge volcano. Scientists think Mercury's volcanoes are extinct.

Directions: Answer the following questions. If you need more space to write an answer, write your answer on your own paper.

161 Which two features compared in the table best explain why Mercury's high temperature is much greater than Earth's?

A Average Distance from Sun and Full Day

B Average Distance from Sun and Number of Moons

C Diameter at Equator and Tilt of Axis

D Diameter at Equator and Year

162 The photograph of the volcano on Mercury supports the idea that Mercury's surface is most like the surface of

A the Moon

B the Sun

C Venus

D Earth

163 Which feature of Mercury explains why a compass would work on the surface of the planet?

A It does not have a moon.

B It orbits the Sun.

C It has an iron core.

D It has volcanoes on its surface.

164 Compare the missions of Mariner 10 and Messenger. Explain why Messenger is expected to gather more information than Mariner 10 did.

165 Identify the evidence the author includes in the "Planet of Extremes" section to show that Mercury is a planet of extreme temperatures. How does the wording the author uses to present the facts emphasize the extreme high and low temperatures? Use **two** details from the article to support your answer.

166 The author compares Mercury with places in the United States several times. Why does the author include these comparisons? Include examples of **two** comparisons in your answer.

167 Why is Mercury's iron core so large compared to the rest of the planet? Summarize the **two** theories that might explain this.

168 Why does the author include the section titled "One Discovery: Volcanoes!"? How does this section relate to the rest of the article?

169 The chart in the article provides facts that show some of the differences between Mercury and Earth. Identify **two** differences that you think could be better shown by using a diagram instead of a table. Explain why you chose those differences.

170 Write an essay in which you describe how the Messenger spacecraft may solve some of Mercury's mysteries. Describe at least **two** mysteries in your answer and explain how the Messenger spacecraft could solve them. Use information from the article to support your answer.

Planning Space

You can complete the chart below to help plan your answer.

Mercury's Mysteries

Examples of Mysteries	How the Messenger Spacecraft Could Solve the Mystery
1)	1)
2)	2)
3)	3)

_____

_____

_____

_____

_____

_____

_____

_____

_____

_____

_____

_____

_____

_____

_____

_____

_____

_____

_____

_____

_____

_____

_____

_____

Directions: Read the passage. Then answer the questions that follow it.

My Favorite Fruit? The Olive!

By Andrea Vlahakis

1   I love plums, and I love blueberries. But as delicious as they are, my favorite fruit is—the olive!

2   The first time I ever saw olive trees was when I visited my grandmother in Greece. She lived in the Peloponnesian peninsula, in the deep south of Greece.

3   I couldn't believe that trees could look so old. Really big gnarled trunks seemed out of place with delicate, slim, silver-green leaves. Fossilized olive leaves, found in Greece, date back almost forty thousand years. I didn't know how old the trees I saw were, but they looked as if they were part of a magical forest from a thousand years ago—at least!

4   How old do olive trees really get? In the right climate—like the Mediterranean, with hot, dry summers and mild winters—anywhere from five hundred to fifteen hundred years.

Olives and My Greek Family

5   Olive orchards had been in my grandmother's family for generations. They grew Kalamata olives. Everyone worked in the orchards—parents, grandparents, brothers, and sisters. Even my father worked there.

6   As a boy in Greece in the late 1920s, my father remembers working with his *papouli*, or grandfather, in the family's

orchards. My father helped harvest the olives in late fall, when they turned from an unripe green to purplish black. The workers would lay huge tarps on the ground, then shake the olive branches with sticks to make the ripe olives fall. After harvest-time my father would help his *papouli* prune the trees for the next season.

All About Olives

7   Nothing was wasted. The pruned wood and any dead branches were used for heating. My father carried small branches home by the armfuls.

8   Some of the crop was saved to be cured and eaten. My father remembers that he and his friends used to stuff their pockets with olives to snack on while they walked to school.

9   But the family's olives were also used for oil. First, the olives were pitted and chopped. Then the olive meats were put in a press to squeeze out the oil. My father and his friends visited the presses to watch. The meats left in the press were used to feed the animals. My father remembers that the family's pigs and chickens *loved* olive meats.

10   And the oil? It was used for cooking in place of butter. During World War II, when there was little food, the Greeks ate *bobota*, a cake-like bread made from cornmeal and, you guessed it, olive oil!

11   The oil was also rubbed into the skin to keep it soft, and a few drops in just-washed hair acted as a good conditioner. My grandmother even made her own soap from the oil. It was light brown with a faint aroma of olives.

Olives and Light

12   My grandmother didn't use candles. She put olive oil in a glass with a little water. (Oil is lighter than water and floats to the top.) She had a cork disk, the size of a quarter, with a hole in the

middle, where the wick would go. The hole was edged with metal so the cork wouldn't burn. To make an olive-oil candle, she'd float the disk in the oil and then light the wick. When the oil was used up, the water put out the flame!

13 As you can see, the olive is a very determined fruit from a practically indestructible tree. It has provided food, light, and heat for centuries. Plums and blueberries may be delicious, but give me olives any day.

Olives have a strong connection to light and to Greece. The Olympic Games began in ancient Greece. It is said that a burning olive branch was the first Olympic flame.

Harvesting, Processing, and Curing Olives

14 Today in Greece, from November to mid-March, olives are harvested much the same way they were in my father's day. Yes, some people use machine harvesting, which shakes the trunks and branches. But a lot of people don't. Why? Some of the groves are very old and are on rocky land where machines can't reach. And handpicking guarantees that the olives won't be damaged.

15 The process of getting oil from the olive isn't that much different, either. But the methods are more modern. First, the olives are crushed with mechanical steel grindstones. Then, the meats are spun in a centrifuge at very high speeds to separate the oil from the meats.

16 What about the olives that you eat? You wouldn't want to eat fresh olives because they taste very bitter. They have to be *cured*, or soaked in a saltwater solution (brine), for up to six months. (The brine is changed from time to time.) Olives can also be stored in the brine.

Directions: Answer the following questions. If you need more space to write an answer, write your answer on your own paper.

171 Reread the first paragraph of the article.

> *"I love plums, and I love blueberries. But as delicious as they are, my favorite fruit is—the olive!"*

How does the rest of the article relate to the main idea of this paragraph?

A It provides support to explain why the author has this opinion.

B It compares and contrasts plums, blueberries, and olives.

C It explains why people in different countries have different tastes.

D It describes the health benefits of different types of food.

172 The illustration is included mainly to represent

A the age and history of the olive trees in the orchard

B the large amount of olives produced every season

C the hard work required to harvest the olives each year

D the family enjoying working together in the olive orchard

173 Which of the following would be best to include to summarize the information in the first paragraph of "Olives and Light"?

A timeline

B table

C diagram

D graph

174 Reread paragraph 3 of the article. Explain how the author makes the trees seem ancient. How does this relate to the information in "Olives and My Greek Family"? Use at least **two** details from the article to support your answer.

175 How has modern machinery changed how olives are harvested? Use details from the main article and from "Harvesting, Processing, and Curing Olives" to support your answer.

176 Explain how olives are cured and why curing is necessary. Use at least **two** details from the article to support your answer.

177 As well as being used for food, olives were used for other purposes. Complete the web below by describing some of the other uses for olives.

Olive oil was used to make a type of candle.

Uses for Olives Other than Food

178 In the section "All About Olives," the author states that "nothing was wasted." Which **two** details from this section best support that statement? Explain why you chose those details.

179 How does the author emphasize that growing and using olives is a family activity? Give at least **two** examples from the article to support your answer.

180 The author states at the beginning and end of the article that plums and blueberries are delicious. What is the main feature of olives that makes them better than plums and blueberries? Write an essay in which you explain what benefits olives have compared to other fruits. Use information from the article to support your answer.

Planning Space

You can complete the graphic organizer below to help plan your answer.

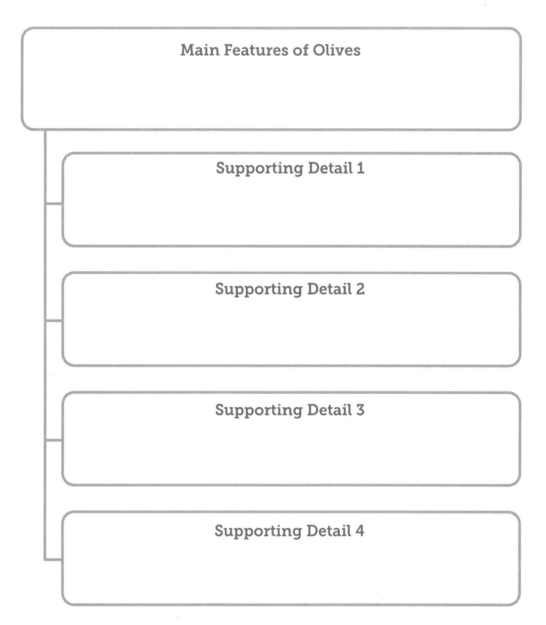

Main Features of Olives

Supporting Detail 1

Supporting Detail 2

Supporting Detail 3

Supporting Detail 4

_____

_____

_____

_____

_____

_____

_____

_____

_____

_____

_____

_____

_____

_____

_____

_____

_____

_____

_____

_____

_____

_____

_____

_____

_____

Part D:

All Together

Literary, Informational, and Paired Passages with Multiple Choice, Short Response, Extended Response, and Essay Questions

Common Core State Standards for Informational Text (Grade 4)

The questions in Part D cover the standards in all three sections of the standards.

Key Ideas and Details: RI.4.1, RI.4.2, RI.4.3

Craft and Structure: RI.4.4, RI.4.5, RI.4.6

Integration of Knowledge and Ideas: RI.4.7, RI.4.8, RI.4.9

Common Core State Standards for Literary Text (Grade 4)

The questions in Part D cover the standards in all three sections of the standards.

Key Ideas and Details: RL.4.1, RL.4.2, RL.4.3

Craft and Structure: RL.4.4, RL.4.5, RL.4.6

Integration of Knowledge and Ideas: RL.4.7, RL.4.9

Directions: Read the passage. Then answer the questions that follow it.

Benny Benson and the Flag Contest

By Martha Whitmore Hickman

1   In Alaska in January, darkness comes early. By the time Benny Benson left school, the stars were already beginning to come out in the night sky.

2   All the way home Benny thought about the contest. His teacher had announced to Benny's seventh-grade class a contest to design a flag—for the whole territory of Alaska. The contest was open to students from seventh grade through high school.

3   The year was 1927. Alaska had been a territory of the United States for more than 14 years and under the U.S. flag for almost 60 years. Now Alaska would have a flag of its own.

4   Benny looked up at the sky. He remembered how his mother had pointed out these same stars when he was a little boy far away from here.

5   Until Benny was three, he and his family had lived in Chignik, a small fishing village in Alaska. Then his mother died, and because his father was a fisherman and had to be away for weeks at a time, Benny went to live at the Jesse Lee Mission Home on the island of Unalaska. During summer, the fields were covered with blue forget-me-nots. In the windy cold winter, some of the villagers lived in cozy *barabaras*, houses dug into the ground with sod for roofs. Then the Home moved to Seward, where there were cows to milk, berries to pick, and trees—and up above, the same stars shining.

Creating His Flag

6   After supper, in his room in the Jesse Lee Mission Home, Benny got out paper and pencil, crayons and paint.

7   What could he draw that would show the Alaska he loved?

8   He thought about the long days of summer, when green plants and flowers grew and only the tops of the mountains still glittered with snow.

9   He thought of the winter, when darkness lasted from late afternoon until after breakfast the next day, when the stars shone brightly in the cold night sky, and when everyone bundled up in fur parkas, mukluks, and mittens.

10 Perhaps he should draw a high mountain, like the mountains around Unalaska or those circling Resurrection Bay? Maybe something about the great bears that trundled around the countryside? Or the tiny blue forget-me-nots that dotted the meadows in spring and summer? Perhaps the deep blue of the Bering Sea, with its fish and its fleets of fishermen? Or the high dome of the sky, with the same stars his mother had pointed out to him when he was a small boy.

11 Slowly, he began to draw. First, he drew the seven stars of the Big Dipper. Then he remembered his mother saying, "Follow the line of the Dipper's outer side, and you'll find the North Star." He drew the North Star.

12 He colored the stars as bright a gold as he could mix. He colored the background the deepest blue.

13 Then he wrote:

> The blue field is for the
> Alaska sky and the forget-me-not,
> an Alaskan flower.
> The North Star is for the
> future state of Alaska, the
> most northerly in the
> union. The Dipper is for
> the Great Bear—symbolizing
> strength.

14   In school, he handed in his design.

Entering the Contest

15   Each local area was to send its best entries to the capital in Juneau. The prize was to be a gold watch with the winning design engraved on the back. The winner wouldn't be announced for several months.

16   The hours of darkness remained long. The weather cold.

17   Winter deepened. Snow fell.

18   Benny and the other children went sledding and tobogganing.

19   Then March came, and vegetation began to grow on the low slopes of the mountains.

The Winner Is Announced

20 One day in March, a messenger brought a telegram to the Jesse Lee Mission School. The superintendent brought it to Benny's seventh-grade classroom and handed it to the teacher.

21 Benny and the others watched as the teacher opened the telegram.

22 She gasped and tried to speak, but she couldn't.

23 The superintendent read the telegram to the class:

> *Flag design by Benny Benson,*
> *Jesse Lee Mission School,*
> *Seward, first place*
> *unanimously. Letter follows—*
> *George A. Parks,*
> *Governor, Territory of Alaska.*

24 The boys and girls jumped from their seats, cheering and shouting. "Benny won! Benny won!"

25 Benny Benson had won the contest!

26 Benny turned pale. His heart pounded. He was too surprised to speak.

27 The whole school was excited about Benny's winning. The superintendent called off classes for the rest of the day.

28 Of course Benny was thrilled that he had won. He was glad, too, when it was time for "lights out" and he could go to the quiet of his room and think about what had happened.

29 For the rest of his life, Benny Benson would be honored as the person who designed the Alaskan flag—which many have called the most beautiful flag of all.

Directions: Answer the following questions. If you need more space to write an answer, write your answer on your own paper.

181 What is the main purpose of the article?

   A to describe what the Alaskan flag looks like

   B to describe how the Alaskan flag was created

   C to explain why Alaska did not have a flag until 1927

   D to compare the flag of Alaska to the flags of other states

182 Which paragraph is included mainly to show that Benny Benson achieved something great?

   A Paragraph 26

   B Paragraph 27

   C Paragraph 28

   D Paragraph 29

183 How were stars important to Benny as a child? Explain what stars meant to him. Use details from the article to support your answer.

184 In paragraph 10, the author asks a series of questions. Explain why the author asks these questions. How does asking questions relate to the main idea of the paragraph? Use details from the article to support your answer.

185 Complete the chart below by describing **three** features of the Alaskan flag. Explain what each feature represents.

Main Features of the Alaskan Flag

Feature	Meaning

186 Compare the reactions of Benny, his teacher, and his classmates to Benny winning the contest. Who seems most shocked by the win? Use at least **two** details from the article to support your answer.

187 The telegram quoted in paragraph 23 uses the word *unanimously*, which means "agreed on by everyone." What does the use of the word show about the success of Benny's design? Use details from the article to support your answer.

188 How does quoting Benny's words in paragraph 13 support the idea that Benny thought carefully about his design? Use details from the article to support your answer.

189 The author includes descriptions of the seasons throughout the article. Explain why the author includes these descriptions. Use at least **two** examples from the article to support your answer.

Planning Space

You can write notes, make a list, or draw a chart to help plan your answer.

_____

_____

_____

_____

_____

_____

_____

_____

_____

_____

_____

_____

_____

_____

190 The article begins with two paragraphs that read like a story. What is the most likely reason the author started the article this way? How might this help readers relate to the article? Use details from the article to support your answer.

Planning Space

You can write notes, make a list, or draw a chart to help plan your answer.

_____

_____

_____

_____

_____

_____

_____

_____

_____

_____

_____

_____

_____

Directions: Read the passage. Then answer the questions that follow it.

The View from Camp

By Clare Mishica

Dear Mother and Dad,

1   My roommate, Syd, may be a problem. He's so sloppy it looks like ten duffel bags exploded in our cabin. He whistles real loud through this gap in his front teeth, too. Plus, he knocked over our lamp and broke it. Syd also wears a funny blue hat for good luck, but I don't think it's working.

Love,
Bryan

Dear Mom and Pop,

2   My roommate, Bryan, seems kind of jumpy, like our cat when you turn on the vacuum cleaner. He hung up a big poster of all the constellations, so maybe he'll teach me how to find them. I'm sure we'll be best buds. Guess what? Our cabin got a brand new lamp.

Love,
Syd

Dear Mother and Dad,

3   Don't worry, but today I almost drowned. We went canoeing across the lake to have a picnic on an island. Halfway there, Syd spotted this fish in the water and dropped his paddle. Before it floated away, I leaned over to grab it, then Syd leaned over, too. We tipped our canoe, and our lunch sank into the muck on the bottom. It felt like I was floating in a giant cup of iced tea! Everything got soaking wet—except for Syd's hat. The other

campers let us borrow some extra clothes, and I had to wear an itchy purple sweatshirt. Syd picked some blueberries for us. He's OK, but I'm probably going to get pneumonia.

Love,
Bryan

Dear Mom and Pop,

4   Today I saw this enormous fish while we were canoeing. The counselor said it might have been a northern pike. I got a real close look before I fell in the lake. My life jacket worked great, and I bobbed up like a cork. The other campers shared all their clothes and food, so I got to meet everyone. Now I have new friends from seven different towns! I'll write more later—I have to help hang up our wet clothes. Bryan has been in a very soggy mood.

Love,
Syd

Dear Mother and Dad,

5   Syd attracts trouble like my giant magnet grabs paper clips. We went for a hike, and Syd stepped on a wasps' nest. The wasps were not happy. The counselor grabbed Syd's hand, and they raced down the trail. The rest of us ran the other way. I got two blisters from running, and poor Syd got stung twice on his face. He said his lucky hat helped him swish most of the wasps away, but that hat mostly brings bad luck. Now Syd has huge chipmunk cheeks. Of course, he can still whistle, but I don't mind anymore.

Love,
Bryan

Dear Mom and Pop,

6   I plan to join the cross-country team this fall. Today I ran half a mile in about three and a half minutes. The counselor said my legs pumped faster than the pistons in his car engine. The wasps that were chasing us probably helped a little. Did you know that some wasps make their nests on the ground? Dad, will you help me train for cross-country when I get home?

Love,
Syd

7   PS: I heard Bryan whistling along with me yesterday. Last night, he showed me the Big Dipper and Orion. Then we made up a new constellation and named it Wasper. We laughed so hard we got the hiccups.

Dear Mother and Dad,

8   Tonight we had a talent show. Syd and I tried to act out *Jack and the Beanstalk*, but Syd accidentally pulled down our rope beanstalk. Everyone laughed, and I wanted to do a disappearing act. Then Syd started telling the campers about our week, and he threw me his lucky hat to act out the stories. Pretty soon, the room was

roaring, and we won first place. Maybe Syd's hat is lucky after all. I had it on last night, and a bunch of campers came to visit. Syd told them I'm a pro with constellations, and they wanted me to point them out. I never made so many friends at one time. I didn't even mind the mess they made in our cabin. I can't believe this, but I'm going to miss Syd.

Love,
Bryan

Dear Mom and Pop,

9   The talent show was fantastic. Bryan really got into it, and we won first place. I may try out for the junior-high play next spring. The counselor told me that I'm a natural onstage and terrific at improvising. At first, I thought that meant yanking down ropes, but it really means making stuff up as you go along.

10   Camp has been the greatest. I was sad to start packing. When Bryan wasn't looking, I put my lucky hat in his bag. He really likes it now, and I want him to have it. Besides, I'm lucky without a hat! See you soon.

Love,
Syd

Directions: Answer the following questions. If you need more space to write an answer, write your answer on your own paper.

191 What does the word *view* in the title most likely refer to?

A how two people saw things that happened

B how one person ruined the camp for another

C how the camp was in a beautiful setting

D how the camp taught people to do new things

192 In paragraph 5, Bryan describes Syd's "huge chipmunk cheeks." What does Bryan mean by this?

A Syd could not stop laughing about what happened.

B Syd started blushing because he was embarrassed.

C Syd had swollen cheeks from the wasp stings.

D Syd keeps telling jokes about the wasps.

193 Reread paragraphs 1 and 2 of the story. What main detail about the new lamp does Syd leave out of his account? What is the most likely reason he leaves it out? Use details from the story to support your answer.

194 Paragraphs 3 and 4 describe the canoeing accident. How is the tone of Syd's account different from the tone of Bryan's account? What does this suggest about what each character is like? Use details from the story to support your answer.

195 A simile is a comparison of two things using the word *like* or *as*. Identify **two** similes Bryan uses in his letters. Explain why Bryan uses each simile.

196 Syd can be described as someone who only sees the best in things. How does Syd's letter describing the wasps illustrate this? Use details from the story to support your answer.

197 How does Bryan feel when things at the talent show first go wrong? How do his feelings change by the end of the talent show? Use details from the story to support your answer.

198 Look closely at the illustration representing the canoeing accident. How can you tell which character is Bryan and which is Syd? Explain what you can tell about how they each feel about falling out of the canoe.

199 How does Bryan feel about Syd's whistling at the beginning and end of the story? Explain how the whistling is used to show Bryan's changing feelings towards Syd. Use details from the story to support your answer.

Planning Space

You can write notes, make a list, or draw a chart to help plan your answer.

200 A main theme of "The View from Camp" is that there are two sides to every story. How does the structure of the story help communicate the theme? Use details from the story to support your answer.

Planning Space

You can write notes, make a list, or draw a chart to help plan your answer.

_____

_____

_____

_____

_____

_____

_____

_____

_____

_____

_____

_____

_____

Directions: Read the passage. Then answer the questions that follow it.

Crimson Harvest:
A Visit to a Cranberry Farm

By Judith Boogaart

1   When winter blows icy cold from the north, Loren House floods his cranberry bogs with water from his small lake. The cranberry vines rest underwater through the long winter. A crust of ice keeps them safe from wind, frost, and snow. But when spring comes and the ice turns to mush and melts, the cranberry bogs come to life.

2   Loren House uses weather forecasts and years of farming know-how to decide when to drain the bogs. Too soon, and a late frost could kill the tender buds. Too late, and the roots would not get the oxygen they need to grow.

3   The thick mat of vines turns reddish brown over the winter. Loren prunes back any old, woody, or overgrown vines before the new shoots appear. Then he feeds them with fertilizer.

4   Soon the sun coaxes the vines to send up new shoots. These short *uprights* sprout shiny green leaves but will not bear fruit this year.

5   In June, buds on last year's shoots open, and the bogs become a carpet of pink-white flowers.

6   Every day, bees buzz among the flowers collecting nectar. The pollen they carry

The Bitter Berry

When Pilgrims first landed in Massachusetts, some of the Algonquin people who lived there shared food with them. Cranberries grew wild in the bogs along the shore, and the natives called them *ibimi*—"bitter berry." When the Pilgrims saw the vines in bloom, the shape of the flowers reminded them of a familiar bird, the crane. They called the fruit "crane-berries," which later became "cranberries."

from blossom to blossom starts the berries growing. When the blossoms fade and drop, the berries begin to appear as little green hubs called *pinheads*.

Tending the Bogs

7   Taking care of the bogs keeps Loren House busy. He checks the spongy soil and irrigates when it is too dry. He weeds out grasses and sedges. He uses a net to sweep the vines for cranberry fruit flies and beetle grubs and decides how to control them. He chooses the best treatment for diseases like root rot and leaf spot.

8   Loren House learned cranberry farming from his father and grandfather. His great-uncle bought this land in 1876, and the family has farmed here ever since. Most cranberries grow in New England, Wisconsin, or the Northwest, but this part of Michigan also has what they need. Winds blowing across Lake Superior keep the weather warmer in winter and cooler in summer. The vines like the sandy, acid soil. And there is plenty of fresh water to irrigate and flood the bogs.

9   Over the next few weeks, the pinheads grow as big as peas and then marbles. They change color from green to pink to red. By October, the berries are crimson, ripe, and ready to pick.

Harvesting the Berries

10   Harvesting is hard work. Some berries are dry harvested. Loren House walks a machine through the dry beds. It has *tines*, like those on a fork. They *comb* the berries off the vines into a box at the back of the machine. The berries then go into a separator. Its blower removes loose vines and leaves. Berries fall down onto small shelves called *bounce boards*. Bad, mushy berries don't bounce; they slide off the shelves to the ground. Only good, firm berries bounce down the shelves to a long tray for final sorting, cleaning, and bagging by hand. Loren House and his wife, Sharon, sell these fresh at their store.

11   Loren House also uses a method called wet harvesting. First he floods the bog until water covers the plants. Then he drives a water-reel harvester through the bog. Its fat tires don't harm the plants. A big reel churns up the water and loosens the berries from the plants. The berries float to the top of the water because they have pockets of air in their centers.

12   Wearing high-wading boots, Loren House and his helpers use floating *boom boards* to gently drag the berries toward a conveyor. His grandsons gather stray berries with butterfly nets.

13   Trucks carry the berries to a machine on the farm for first cleaning. Then they are loaded on big trailers and shipped to another cleaning station and on to the processor.

14   There they become the juice and sauce that show up on our tables.

15   Soon the December winds will howl again. Time for Loren House to put the cranberry bogs to bed for another winter, the way his family has been doing for more than 100 years.

Directions: Answer the following questions. If you need more space to write an answer, write your answer on your own paper.

201 What does the word *crimson* in the title of the article refer to?

   A where cranberries got their name from

   B where the cranberries are grown

   C what cranberries taste like

   D what cranberries look like

202 All of the following sentences support the idea that the cranberry farm is a family business EXCEPT

   A "Loren House uses weather forecasts and years of farming know-how to decide when to drain the bogs."

   B "Loren House learned cranberry farming from his father and grandfather."

   C "Loren House and his wife, Sharon, sell these fresh at their store."

   D "His grandsons gather stray berries with butterfly nets."

203 The article describes how the bogs are drained each year. Why is it important that the bogs are drained at the right time? Use details from the article to support your answer.

204 The section "Harvesting the Berries" describes how bounce boards are used in the harvesting. Explain how the bounce boards sort the berries. Use details from the article to support your answer.

205 Read this sentence from the last paragraph of the article.

> *"Time for Loren House to put the cranberry bogs to bed for another winter, the way his family has been doing for more than 100 years."*

Explain what the author means by "put the cranberry bogs to bed." Use details from the article to support your answer.

206 The section titled "Tending the Bogs" tells how Loren House has to solve problems to keep the cranberry plants healthy. Complete the graphic organizer below by describing **two** problems and how they are solved.

Problem		Solution
	→	

Problem		Solution
	→	

207 What does the section "The Bitter Berry" describe? Explain why the author included this section. Use details from the article to support your answer.

208 The photograph shows a process described in the article. Use details from the article to write a summary of the process shown.

209 In "Harvesting the Berries," the author states that "harvesting is hard work." Does the author include enough details to support this statement? Use details from the article to support your answer.

Planning Space

You can write notes, make a list, or draw a chart to help plan your answer.

_____

_____

_____

_____

_____

_____

_____

_____

_____

_____

_____

_____

_____

_____

_____

_____

210 The cranberries can be harvested by dry harvesting or wet harvesting. Compare how the berries harvested each way are used. Why do you think the berries harvested each way are used for different purposes? Use details from the article to support your answer.

Planning Space

You can write notes, make a list, or draw a chart to help plan your answer.

_____

_____

_____

_____

_____

_____

_____

_____

_____

_____

_____

_____

_____

Directions: Read the following two passages. Then answer the questions that follow.

Ready

By James Price

1 Five seconds to go.
Two points behind.
Standing just beyond
the three-point line.

2 Should I call for it?
What if I miss it?
Can I do it?

3 "Here! Here!"
The ball is mine.
The chance is mine.
The game could be ours.

4 No time to think.
Just shoot.
My body acts
while my mind races.

5 The ball soars
towards the net.

6 Bodies pause in mid-step.
Faces turn in slow motion.
Silence.

7 It sails through.
Three points.
The win.

8 My team cheers.
The other team sighs.
"Lucky shot," someone mumbles.

9 No. Not luck.
Hours of work.
Hours of practice.
Hours preparing for one moment.
And I was ready
for that moment.
I did it.
I don't remember how
but I did it.

Making a Lay-Up

By Anthony F. Stump

1   The lay-up is the most basic shot in basketball. Professional players have to make lay-ups at full speed with defenders trying to block the shot. But you can practice alone, as long as you know how to do it.

2   When you practice a skill enough times, it becomes automatic. To make a lay-up, you'll be jumping off one foot while shooting with the opposite hand. Your shooting hand will be the one farther from the basket, making it difficult for a defender to block the shot.

3   The best way to learn a skill like this one is to break it into smaller steps, learning to shoot the ball first and then adding footwork and dribbling.

The Angle Shot

4   Stand to the right of the basket, about three feet away. With your elbow bent, hold the ball in your right hand. Lift that hand so it's next to your head with the palm up. Tilt your wrist backward and let the ball rest on the pads of your fingers, not in your palm. Steady the ball with your left hand and bend your knees. Keep your eyes on the square on the backboard. Aim for the top corner of the square (the side closest to you) and launch the ball. Your goal is to bank the ball into the basket by bouncing it off the backboard.

Step and Shoot

5   Stand about six feet from the basket this time and take a large step with your left foot. That foot will land about where you were standing for the angle shot. As your left foot reaches that spot, jump off it and make the shot with your right hand. (You'll

be bending your right knee as you jump.) That's how to make a right-handed lay-up.

Footwork

6   After you've mastered the one-step lay-up, move several feet farther back. Dribble with your right hand. Make your last step with your left foot, jumping up and forward with that foot and taking the shot with your right hand. At first, you might need to take a few short steps in order to reach the proper spot for the left-footed jump. Practice dribbling slowly, then increase your speed as you get the hang of it. The faster you approach the basket, the "softer" your shot needs to be.

Double Your Skill

7   You can use these same steps for left-side lay-ups, but use the opposite hand and foot. Jump with the right foot and shoot with the left hand.

8   By learning to shoot from both sides and with both hands, you'll become a much more effective player.

9   Remember that you can improve most athletic skills by thinking about the action. Picture yourself making a lay-up with proper form, jumping off the correct foot. The more you practice, the easier it will be for your brain to remember. Soon you'll be doing it automatically.

10   Now go practice!

Directions: Use "Ready" to answer the following questions. If you need more space to write an answer, write your answer on your own paper.

211 What do the lines in the second stanza represent?

    A things that people in the crowd yell

    B what the speaker worries about

    C how the other players make the speaker feel

    D questions the coach asks of the players

212 Which line best helps the reader imagine how nervous the speaker feels?

    A "The chance is mine."

    B "No time to think."

    C "while my mind races."

    D "The ball soars"

213 How is the poem different from prose? What features show that "Ready" is a poem? Use details from the poem to support your answer.

214 Think about what the purpose of the poem is. Does the first-person point of view help the poem achieve its purpose? Use details from the poem to support your conclusion.

215 Read these lines from the poem.

"Bodies pause in mid-step.
Faces turn in slow motion."

What are these two lines describing? How do the two lines show how the players feel? Use details from the poem to support your answer.

Directions: Use "Making a Lay-Up" to answer the following questions. If you need more space to write an answer, write your answer on your own paper.

216 The author uses subheadings to divide the information into sections. Describe how the sections "The Angle Shot," "Step and Shoot," and "Footwork" fit together. Use details from the article to support your answer.

217 The article shows that it takes practice to perfect a lay-up. Using information from the article, explain why it would be worthwhile for a player to perfect the shot. Use at least **two** reasons to support your answer.

218 Is the main purpose of the passage to instruct, inform, or encourage? Use details from the article to support your answer.

Directions: Use both "Ready" and "Making a Lay-Up" to answer the following questions.

219 Read these sentences from the end of the article.

> *"The more you practice, the easier it will be for your brain to remember. Soon you'll be doing it automatically."*

How do these sentences relate to the speaker in the poem? Use details from the poem and the article to support your answer.

Planning Space

You can write notes, make a list, or draw a chart to help plan your answer.

_____

_____

_____

_____

_____

_____

_____

_____

_____

_____

_____

_____

220 The poem and the article are both about practicing basketball skills. Compare how each passage shows the importance of practicing. Which passage do you think would most make a player want to practice new skills? Use details from the poem and the article to support your answer.

Planning Space

You can complete the chart below to help plan your answer.

	Ready	Making a Lay-Up
How are the ideas presented?		
How does it show the importance of practicing?		
Would it make players want to practice?		

_____

_____

_____

_____

_____

_____

_____

_____

_____

_____

_____

_____

Directions: Read the passage. Then answer the questions that follow it.

Going in Circles Around Saturn

By Ken Croswell, Ph.D.

1   Saturn is spectacular, boasting bright and beautiful rings. You can see the rings through a telescope.

2   The edge of the outside main ring is a huge circle 170,000 miles across. That's nearly three-fourths of the distance from Earth to the Moon. But the rings are just 30 feet thick. You could walk such a short distance in a few seconds.

3   The rings are made of trillions of ice particles going around Saturn. Some of the ice particles are as small as marbles; others are as big as horses and houses.

4   Saturn is the Sun's only planet with brilliant rings. Jupiter, Uranus, and Neptune also have rings, but their rings are dark and hard to see. All of these planets are giants, much larger than Earth.

What Made the Rings?

5   Where did Saturn's rings come from? People have wondered for hundreds of years, ever since astronomers discovered the rings.

6   But now Robin Canup, Ph.D., may have solved the puzzle. She's a scientist at the Southwest Research Institute in Boulder, Colorado, and she uses computers to see what happens when planets and moons interact with one another.

7   Dr. Canup thinks Saturn's rings formed when a big moon smashed into the planet.

Planets Rock!

8   Dr. Canup became interested in astronomy long ago. "Back in second grade, part of our science book was on the Moon and the planets," she says. "I liked thinking about whether there were other planets that might have life on them."

9   There's no life on Saturn.

10 The planet is too far from the Sun and too cold. But Saturn was her favorite planet. "It is stunningly beautiful," she says.

11 Saturn has more than just incredible rings. It also has 62 moons, or satellites. They go around Saturn just as the Moon goes around Earth. One of Saturn's satellites, named Titan, is bigger than our Moon. Titan is even bigger than Mercury and Pluto. Many of Saturn's moons, including Titan, formed in a disk of gas and dust that went around Saturn billions of years ago, when Saturn was young.

A Possible Solution

12 Dr. Canup thinks she can solve the mystery of Saturn's rings. She has an interesting idea, or hypothesis, about how the rings formed.

13 She thinks that once, long ago, Saturn had another large moon just like Titan. After the Titan-like moon formed, it spiraled through the disk of gas and dust, moving closer and closer to Saturn, until the moon crashed into the planet.

14   Like Titan, the moon was half rock and half ice. The rock was at the moon's center. The ice was on the surface.

15   "As the moon got very close to Saturn, the gravity of Saturn was strong enough to begin to strip material from it," Dr. Canup says.

16   That's because gravity causes tides. A tide occurs when gravity pulls harder on one side of an object than on the other side. For example, the Moon's gravity pulls Earth's seas up and down.

17   In the same way, Saturn's tides yanked on the big moon's ice. As the moon moved closer to Saturn, it passed through the Roche limit. The Roche limit is where a planet's tides tear things to shreds.

18   "So Saturn's gravity stripped ice from the satellite," says Dr. Canup. "The planet started peeling off the outer layers of the satellite, but the satellite was continuing to spiral inwards." Dr. Canup thinks the ice particles went into orbit around Saturn and became the rings.

Plunging into Saturn

19   However, Dr. Canup says, Saturn's tides didn't tear up the moon's rocky core. Because rock is denser than ice, the core resisted Saturn's tides. The rock plunged into Saturn. In the moon's place were glorious rings of ice, with almost no rock.

20   Dr. Canup's idea agrees with all the laws of planetary motion. But to test her idea, she needs to study more planets with big, bright rings.

21   Giant planets go around many stars besides the Sun. Maybe some of those planets have rings as spectacular as Saturn's. If so, then Dr. Canup may be able to see whether their rings were made by large moons that crashed into their planets.

The Birth of Saturn's Rings

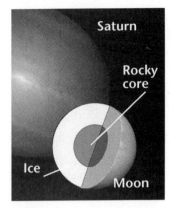

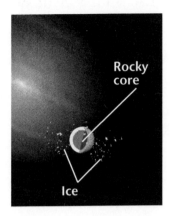

Where did Saturn's spectacular rings come from? Dr. Canup's idea may solve the mystery.

Billions of years ago, Saturn was bigger than it is today. Dr. Canup thinks it had an icy moon with a rocky core.

If such a moon crossed the Roche limit, Saturn's powerful gravity would have peeled off the moon's ice layer.

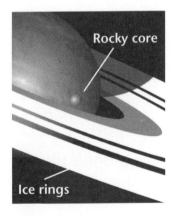

Trillions of ice pieces would have gone into orbit around Saturn, forming wide, flat rings.

The rocky core of the moon would have plunged into Saturn, leaving the rings behind.

Directions: Answer the following questions. If you need more space to write an answer, write your answer on your own paper.

221 Read this sentence from the article.

> *"After the Titan-like moon formed, it spiraled through the disk of gas and dust, moving closer and closer to Saturn, until the moon crashed into the planet."*

What does the word *spiraled* suggest about the moon?

A It shone brightly.

B It moved slowly.

C It was out of control.

D It was hard to see.

222 According to the article, how will Dr. Canup find evidence to support her theory?

A by observing Saturn's largest moon, Titan

B by studying other planets with bright rings

C by comparing the rings of all the giant planets

D by collecting data on Saturn using computers

223 How are the rings of Jupiter, Uranus, and Neptune different from Saturn's rings?

A They are older.

B They are wider.

C They are dimmer.

D They are rockier.

224 Paragraph 3 explains that Saturn's rings are "made of trillions of ice particles." How does this fact support Dr. Canup's theory? Use details from the article to support your answer.

225 How are the author's and Dr. Canup's feelings about Saturn similar? Use at least **two** specific details from the article to show how the author and Dr. Canup feel about Saturn.

226 Reread paragraph 3 of the article. Explain why the author compares the ice particles to marbles, horses, and houses. Use details from the article to support your answer.

227 In the section "Planets Rock!," the author quotes Dr. Canup. Explain the purpose of the quotes and describe the background information they give. Use details from the article to support your answer.

228 The third diagram in "The Birth of Saturn's Rings" refers to the Roche limit. Explain what the Roche limit is. What is the difference between a moon orbiting outside the Roche limit and a moon orbiting inside the Roche limit? Use details from the article to support your answer.

229 The last diagram in "The Birth of Saturn's Rings" shows how the rocky core plunged into Saturn. What does the diagram show about what happened when the rocky core hit Saturn? How does this explain why there would not be rock in the planet's rings? Use details from the article to support your answer.

230 The diagrams are included to show how Saturn's rings formed. Using the diagrams as a guide, write a summary of the events that occurred to form Saturn's rings. Use information from the diagrams and the main article in your answer.

Planning Space

You can complete the chart below to help plan your answer.

How Saturn's Rings Formed

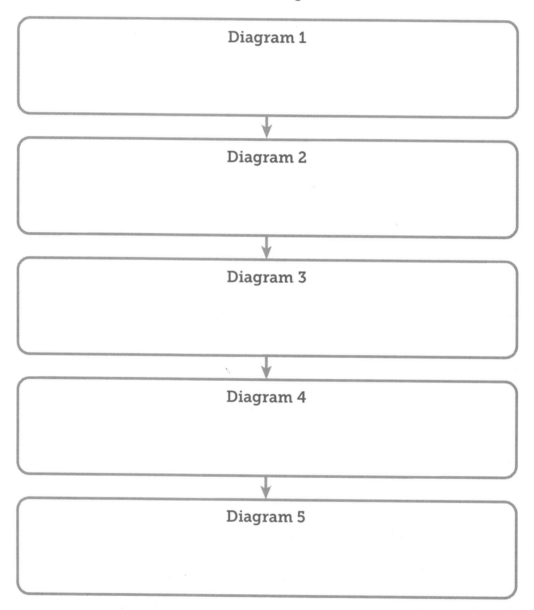

Directions: Read the following two passages. Then answer the questions that follow.

Little Mo

By James M. Janik

1   Montgomery Ashford got his nickname back in sixth grade.

2   While the rest of us doubled in size the summer before middle school, Little Mo still had to sit on his feet to see at the movies. When we'd take turns jumping for the rim during basketball in gym class, Little Mo needed a boost to nick the net with a fingertip. Little Mo was, well, little.

3   Most guys would waste their time whining about such a lousy break. It's tough to fit in when you're looking up at everyone's chin most of the time. Little Mo never complained. In fact, he saw his shortness as a positive. He was funny that way. Once you knew him and how he saw things, it was impossible to feel sorry for him.

4   For most of the year, especially during football and basketball seasons, Little Mo avoided attention. Keeping "under the radar" is what he called it. When March rolled around, things changed. Little Mo lived for the spotlight of baseball season.

5   At the start of the first game, the opposing team slung the usual insults. Little Mo just smiled. All the kids on our bench folded their arms, waiting.

6   After the pitcher and catcher finished their giggling and snickering and got down to the business of pitching, their smirks faded.

7   Little Mo dug in the batter's box, the sleeves of his jersey hanging down past his elbows.

8   Now, the typical strike zone is a nice big rectangle. Home plate is 17 inches wide, and most 12-year-olds have a workable distance between their knees and their armpits. When Little Mo crouched, his rectangle seemed to fold up like a road map. From the pitcher's mound, Little Mo's strike zone looked like a mail slot.

9   The catcher squatted as low as he could, but his mitt still made too high a target. He tried lying down but couldn't find any place to stick his fingers to call pitches. Finally, he kneeled on the ground and hoped he wouldn't have to go anywhere in a hurry.

10   The pitcher squinted, searching for some reasonable place to throw the ball. But there was no reasonable place. Little Mo got his walk on four pitches every time he was up. He dropped his bat and ran to first base.

11   Little Mo's height advantage didn't stop there. You might think running fast on such short legs would be impossible. But you'd only think that if you never saw a millipede zip across the kitchen floor or a chipmunk dash from the flower bed to the weed line. Short legs make for small steps, but short steps take less time to make.

12 Giving up a walk to Little Mo was the same as giving up a triple. The next hitter only had to watch two pitches go by, and Little Mo would steal second, then third. Before the pitcher knew what had happened, Little Mo would be standing on third, waiting to score.

13 Little Mo set all sorts of league records. He started every All Star game. He was a run-scoring machine.

14 By the end of the season, we all wished we weren't quite so tall. Our strike zones were enormous! It took forever for our long legs to carry us to second base on a steal.

15 Little Mo grinned whenever we mentioned how lucky he was to be so short and fast. He agreed that he was lucky to get so much attention but never rubbed it in. He was funny that way.

16 His luck ended the year he turned thirteen.

17 Little Mo went off to summer camp right after our last game. As always, he'd led the league in walks, steals, and runs scored. When he came back from camp, he'd grown six inches. His voice had dropped about three octaves. We didn't recognize him. His mom called it a growth spurt. We called it a disaster. We'd lost the best lead-off hitter in the league's history! What a lousy break.

18 But Little Mo didn't see it like that. He said he'd always wanted to give basketball a try. And he thought he might like to try wide receiver, too. We just scratched our heads. He was funny that way.

Fishing for Gold

By Teresa Bateman

1   Everyone agreed that Eamon was the laziest leprechaun in all of Ireland.

2   While other leprechauns were cobbling, playing the harp, dancing, or practicing magic, what was Eamon doing? Fishing! Who ever heard of a leprechaun that fished?

3   Since fishing took up all his time, Eamon couldn't make a shoe, play a tune, or dance a jig. And magic? Well, that was a complete disaster.

4   The other leprechauns shook their heads.

5   "You need to practice harder."

6   "You need to study harder."

7   "You need to try harder."

8   But Eamon didn't want to. He loved to fish, and he was good at it. He had only to cast his line and fish came leaping to his bait.

9   "It's a tasty talent," his friends said, laughing, "but magic can put food on the table with less effort. And it's magic you'll need to be a true leprechaun."

10 Eamon knew that this was so. Soon he'd be given a pot of gold. Gold strengthened leprechaun magic, and according to law each leprechaun of a certain age had to guard a pot of it.

11 The safest place to hide this leprechaun gold was at the end of a rainbow—where only leprechaun magic could reach. Unfortunately, Eamon's magic was so weak, he couldn't get to the end of a rainbow.

12 "You need to practice harder."

13 "You need to study harder."

14 "You need to try harder."

15 So he did. He cobbled ill-fitting shoes, strummed his harp while the neighbors held their ears, and stepped on the toes of any partner willing to risk a dance with him.

16 And he practiced magic. But he couldn't get the magic to work.

17 To raise his spirits, Eamon walked to the brook one sunlit morning. He cast his fishing line as he cast his mind in search of a solution. Then, gazing at his favorite waterfall, he suddenly knew what to do.

18 The day arrived to go before the throne.

19 "This is leprechaun gold," the king said solemnly, placing the gleaming pot before Eamon. "Can you keep it safe?"

20 The young leprechaun nodded. "I will place it at the end of a rainbow and retrieve it when there's need."

21 After the ceremony, Eamon hid his gold.

22 Summer arrived— the hottest one Ireland had known. The skies were steely blue with nary a cloud, and the grass withered on the hills.

23 With no rain, there could be no rainbows. With no rainbows, it was impossible for the leprechauns to reach their treasure.

24   As the days of drought continued, magic in the community
      faded. The leprechauns grew thinner, for magic had helped put
      food on their tables. Eamon's fishing became more than a hobby
      as he began feeding his friends and neighbors.

25   Dry days turned to dry weeks. Then one day a sentry came
      running into the village square.

26   "There are men in our valley!" he cried.

27   Usually this would have been a small problem. The leprechauns
      would use magic to lead the men away, but their magic had
      worn thin as a thimble.

28   Eamon knew what he had to do. He hurried to the king's throne
      and bowed. "Might leprechaun gold help?"

29   The king frowned. "Gold would help, but how can we find the
      end of a rainbow without rain?"

30   Eamon hesitated. "I hid my gold, as I said."

31   The king nodded.

32   "I'd better show you," Eamon continued.

33 The king followed Eamon to the waterfall. "You didn't hide it at the end of a rainbow trout, did you?" he joked.

34 Eamon chuckled nervously, then pointed. Smaller due to the drought, the waterfall still sent out enough spray for the sun to spread a rainbow in the mist. Eamon reached in and pulled out his pot of gold.

35 The king smiled. "You're a clever leprechaun. You followed the law, in your own way, and it's lucky you did. Your gold can keep everyone safe until the rains return."

36 So he said, and so it was. Each leprechaun took a gold coin from the pot. Together, they used their magic to befuddle the intruders. The village was safe again.

37 There was a great celebration—a fine fish dinner, of course.

38 Eamon continued to share his gold and his fish until the rains fell. Nobody laughed at him anymore, and everyone came to him for fishing lessons.

39 Few, however, were willing to put in the time and energy fishing required.

40 "You need to practice harder, study harder, and try harder," Eamon told them, but he said it with a twinkle in his eye. "Well, we all have our talents. Go ahead and chase your rainbows. Just let me chase mine in my own way."

Directions: Use "Little Mo" to answer the following questions. If you need more space to write an answer, write your answer on your own paper.

231 What do the details in paragraph 3 mainly show about Little Mo?

A He gets upset easily.

B He does not stand up for himself.

C He has a good sense of humor.

D He is relaxed and easygoing.

232 The author describes Little Mo as a "run-scoring machine." What does the word *machine* mainly suggest?

A Little Mo scores runs without thinking.

B Little Mo is good at scoring runs.

C Little Mo scores runs the same way every time.

D Little Mo is tired of scoring so many runs.

233 The narrator of the story helps the reader understand Little Mo mainly by

A describing his actions

B quoting his speech

C telling his emotions

D showing his problems

234 Look closely at the illustration of Little Mo and the catcher on page 271. Describe how Little Mo and the catcher seem to feel. How does this support information in the story? Use details from the story to support your answer.

235 Read these sentences from paragraph 8 of the story.

> *"When Little Mo crouched, his rectangle seemed to fold up like a road map. From the pitcher's mound, Little Mo's strike zone looked like a mail slot."*

Are the similes an effective way to emphasize how hard it was to pitch to Little Mo? Use details from the story to support your answer.

Directions: Use "Fishing for Gold" to answer the following questions. If you need more space to write an answer, write your answer on your own paper.

236 Why is the lack of rain important in the story? How does it lead to Eamon needing to use his talents? Use details from the story to support your answer.

237 Read this dialogue spoken by the king.

> *"You're a clever leprechaun. You followed the law, in your own way, and it's lucky you did. Your gold can keep everyone safe until the rains return."*

How does this dialogue summarize the main lesson of the story? Use details from the story to support your answer.

238 At the beginning of the story, the other leprechauns think Eamon is lazy. How does the view of Eamon change by the end of the story? What causes their views to change? Use details from the story to support your answer.

239 Read these sentences from the last paragraph.

> *"You need to practice harder, study harder, and try harder," Eamon told them, but he said it with a twinkle in his eye.*

What does the phrase "with a twinkle in his eye" show about Eamon? What can you infer about how he feels? Use details from the story to support your conclusion.

Directions: Use both "Little Mo" and "Fishing for Gold" to answer the following question.

240 Everyone has both strengths and weaknesses. Think about how Little Mo and Eamon each have strengths and weaknesses. Write an essay in which you describe how the characters Little Mo and Eamon both show the importance of being yourself and making the most of who you are. Use information from both stories to support your answer.

Planning Space

You can complete the chart below to help plan your answer.

	Little Mo	Eamon
Strengths		
Weaknesses		
Using Strengths and Weaknesses		

_____

_____

_____

_____

_____

_____

_____

_____

_____

_____

_____

_____

_____

_____

_____

_____

_____

_____

_____

_____

_____

_____

_____

_____

_____

_____

_____